An
Edgar Allan Poe
Reader

AN ADAPTED CLASSIC

An
Edgar Allan Poe
Reader

EDGAR ALLAN POE

GLOBE FEARON
Pearson Learning Group

Ollie Depew
formerly Professor of English
Southern Oregon College of Education
Ashland, Oregon

Herbert Spencer Robinson
formerly Adjunct Professor of English
Pace University, New York

Cover Design: Marek Antoniak
Cover Illustration: Robert Pasternak
Text Illustrations: Vivian Berger, Ted Burwell, Joe Forté,
Ron Jones, Bruce Waldman

ISBN 0-835-90243-9

Printed in the United States of America
27 28 29 30 V313 11

1-800-321-3106
www.pearsonlearning.com

About the Author

Edgar Allan Poe was born in Boston, Massachusetts in 1809. Both of his parents had died by the time he was three. He was adopted by Mr. and Mrs. John Allan of Richmond, Virginia, where he lived until 1827. He was sent to school in England and Richmond. Poe then spent a year at the University of Virginia before he enlisted in the army. Between 1827 and 1831 he published three volumes of poetry. In 1833 he won a short story competition. He later worked on magazines in Richmond, New York, and Philadelphia, writing stories, poems, essays, and book reviews. Many of his most famous stories, including "The Fall of the House of Usher," were written for these magazines. He won another short story competition with "The Gold Bug" in 1843. It was at this time that Poe first developed the mystery story, including "The Murders in the Rue Morgue." By January of 1845, when his poem "The Raven" was published, Poe had become the most talked-about writer of his time. He died in October 1849.

Poe is still considered one of the greatest American writers. His short stories are famous all over the world. These stories have earned him the title of Father of the Short Story in America.

Poe is also the Father of the Detective Story. His detective, Dupin, later became a model for another famous detective, Sherlock Holmes, created by Arthur Conan Doyle.

Edgar Allan Poe also wrote some of the greatest poetry in American literature. His poems are full of magic, mystery, melody, and beautiful sounds.

Finally, the literary essays and book reviews he wrote have won Poe another title, Father of Literary Criticism in America.

Preface

The stories selected for this collection are grouped under four headings: Mystery, Horror and Fear, the Psychological, and the Humorous.

Stories of Mystery open the collection. In these stories Poe displays his interest in studying, solving, and even inventing, problems. He enjoyed using his mind to clear up a mystery, to break a code, or to solve a crime. Poe's French detective, Dupin, appears in "The Murders in the Rue Morgue" and "The Purloined Letter." These are first-class detective stories. They, like "The Gold Bug" are also stories of analysis. Poe called them tales of *ratiocination,* or stories of logical reasoning. Dupin solves crimes, and Legrand breaks a code, by using the power of reasoning.

Stories of Horror and Fear deal with death, revenge, and cruelty. These are among Poe's favorite subjects, used by him again and again. Tales such as "The Black Cat" and "The Cask of Amontillado" create atmosphere, which Poe felt was even more important than creating character. "A Descent Into the Maelstrom" and "The Pit and the Pendulum" are horror stories. The first deals with the horrors of nature. The second deals with the horrors used by people to torture their enemies.

The Psychological Stories probe beneath the surface of a person's mind, character, and personality. "William Wilson" is especially interesting because it deals with what is known as a double, or dual, personality. Robert Louis Stevenson's *The Strange Case of Dr. Jekyll and Mr. Hyde* deals with a similar theme.

The Humorous Stories reveal a side of Poe that is not always remembered. Poe was a strange, unhappy personality. He often seemed to be as strange as any character he ever created. But he had a sense of humor all his own. It was as original and as far removed from the usual as his sense of beauty and mystery. This side of him is shown in several stories in this collection, including "Never Bet the Devil Your Head."

As a poet, Poe was mainly interested in the sounds of words and word combinations. The themes of his poetry include love, beauty, death, and romance. All of his poems are purposely short. Poe believed that there was no such thing as a long poem. He even went so far as to say that a long poem was simply several short poems with bad or weak spots between the good ones. Some of his most famous poems, including "The Raven" which brought him his first big success, are included in this collection.

This book, then, contains some of the stories and poems that have made Edgar Allan Poe a world figure and that have given pleasure to readers for almost 150 years.

Adapter's Note

In preparing this edition of AN EDGAR ALLAN POE READER, we have kept the author's main purpose in mind. However, language has changed since the stories and poems were originally published. We have modified or omitted some passages and vocabulary in the stories. We have, however, kept as much of the original language as possible.

Contents

STORIES OF MYSTERY

The Gold Bug
The Murders in the Rue Morgue
The Purloined Letter

The Gold Bug

Many years ago I grew to know and to like William Legrand. He was once wealthy, but had lost most of his property. After he became poor, he left his old home in New Orleans and went to live on Sullivan's Island, near Charleston, South Carolina.

This island, made of little else but sea sand, is about three miles long. At no point is it wider than a quarter of a mile. It is separated from the mainland by a small creek that oozes its way through reeds and slime. The whole island, except the western point where Fort Moultrie stands, was covered thickly with shrubs. Near the eastern or more lonely end of the island, Legrand had built himself a small hut, and was living there when I came to know him.

We soon became friends. I found him well-educated, with unusual powers of mind, but moody. He had many books about, but rarely used them. He liked to hunt and fish, or to saunter along the beach looking for shells, of which he had a fine collection. With him lived his black man called Jupiter, an old family servant, who would not leave "young Master Will" now that he was poor.

Just before sunset, in the middle of October, 18—, I scrambled my way through the shrubs to the hut of my friend Legrand. I had not visited him for several weeks. My home at that time was in Charleston, only nine miles from the island, but means of travel were far behind those of the present day. Upon reaching the hut, I rapped, but got no reply. I then looked for the key where I knew it was kept, unlocked the door and went in. The winters on Sullivan's Island are very mild, and in the fall a fire is not often needed. But this day had been chilly, and I found a fine fire blazing on the hearth. I took an armchair by the crackling logs, and waited for my friend to return.

Soon after dark he and Jupiter came, and I received a most hearty welcome. Jupiter, grinning from ear to ear, bustled about to prepare some marsh hens for supper. Legrand was in one of his cheerful moods. He had found an unknown shell, and more than this, he had with Jupiter's help, caught a strange beetle, perhaps as yet unknown to science. He would show it to me, he said, in the morning.

"And why not tonight?" I asked, rubbing my hands over the blaze, and really caring very little about any beetle.

"Ah, if I had only known you were here!" said Legrand. "As I was coming home, I met Lieutenant G——from the fort, and I lent him the bug. But stay here tonight and I will send Jup down for it at sunrise. It is a beautiful gold color, about the size of a large hickory nut, with two jet-black spots near one end of the back, and another spot somewhat larger at the other end. The antennae[1] are—"

"There ain't no *tin* in him, Master Will," broke in Jupiter. "I keep a-tellin' you that. The bug is a *gold* bug, solid, every bit of him, inside and all, 'cept his wing—never feel half so heavy a bug in my life."

"Well, suppose it is, Jup," said Legrand; "but don't let the birds burn. The color—" here he turned to me—"is really very like gold. Wait, let me give you some idea of its shape." He seated himself at a small table and looked about for some paper, but found none. "This will do," he said, and drew from his waistcoat pocket a scrap of what looked like very

---

[1] Plural form of "antenna," a feeler or horn of an insect.

heavy and dirty paper. He set to work, making a rough drawing of the beetle.

While he was making the drawing, I kept my seat by the fire, for I was still chilly. When it was done, he handed it to me without rising. As I took it, a scratching was heard at the door. Jupiter opened it, and a large dog belonging to Legrand came in. The dog jumped upon me with joy, for I had paid him much attention on other visits. When his playing was over, I looked at the paper, and to speak the truth, was a little puzzled by what I saw.

"Well!" I said, "this *is* a strange beetle—new to me—never saw anything like it before—unless it was a skull or death's-head."[2]

"A death's-head!" said Legrand. "Ah—yes—well, the drawing does look a little like one. The two upper black spots look like eyes, eh? And the larger one at the other end looks like a mouth. And then the shape of the whole is oval."

"But, Legrand, I fear you are no artist. I must wait until I see the beetle itself. Where are the antennae you spoke of?" I asked, still looking at the strange drawing.

"The antennae!" said Legrand, who was beginning to be vexed. "I am sure you must see the antennae. I made them as plain as they are on the beetle, and that should be plain enough."

"Well, well," I said, "perhaps you have—still I don't see them."

I handed him the paper without saying more, not wishing to ruffle his temper further. But on this drawing, there were certainly no antennae to be seen, and the whole *did* look very like the usual drawing of a death's-head.

He took the paper and was about to crumple it, as if to throw it into the fire, when something in the drawing caught his eye. His face flushed red—then went pale. For some minutes he sat looking closely at the drawing. At last

---

[2] A skull, an emblem of death.

3

he rose, took a candle from the table, and went to sit on a sea chest in the farthest corner of the room. Here again he looked closely at the paper, turning it in all directions. He said nothing, however, and I did not wish to arouse his moody temper by any remarks.

Soon he took from his coat pocket a wallet, placed the paper carefully in it, and put the wallet in a writing desk, which he locked. His manner now became pleasant again, but his old air of cheerfulness was quite gone. Yet he seemed not so much sulky as thoughtful. As the evening wore away, he went more and more into silent thought, from which no talk of mine could rouse him.

I had meant to pass the night at the hut, as I had often done before, but seeing him in this mood, I thought best to take leave. He did not press me to stay, but as I left he shook my hand with even more than his usual good will.

It was about a month after this (during which I had not seen Legrand) when I had a visit in Charleston, from his man Jupiter. I had never seen him look so downhearted.

"Well, Jup," I said, "what is the matter now? How is your master?"

"Why, to speak the truth, him not so very well as might be."

"Not well! I am sorry to hear it. What does he complain of?"

"There! That is it!—him never 'plain of nothin'—but him very sick for all that."

"*Very* sick—why didn't you say so at once! Is he in bed all the time? Hasn't he told you what he suffers from?"

"Master Will say nothin' at all's the matter with him. But then what make him go about looking this here way, with he head down and he shoulders up, and as white as a ghost? And then he keeps making figures all de time. I is gettin' to be scared, I tell you. The other day he give me the slip 'fore sunup and was gone the whole blessed day. And he look so very poorly."

"And you have no idea of what caused this? Has anything unpleasant happened since I was there?"

"No, sir, not *since* then—it was 'fore then, I'm feared. It was the very day you was there."

"What do you mean?"

"I mean the bug."

"The what?"

"The bug—I'm very certain that Master Will been bit somewhere 'bout the head by that gold bug."

"And why do you think so, Jupiter?"

"I never did see such a bug—he kick and he bite every t'ing what come near him. When Master Will firs' catch him, he had to let him go again mighty quick, I tell you. Then was the time he must ha' got the bite. I didn't like the look of the bug's mouth, myself. I wouldn't take hold of him with my fingers, but I catch him with a piece of paper that I found."

"And you think, then, that your master was bitten by the beetle, and that the bite made him sick?"

"I knows it. What make him dream 'bout gold so much, if it ain't 'cause he bit by the gold bug? I heared 'bout them gold bugs 'fore now."

"Did you bring any word from Mr. Legrand?"

"No, sir, I bring this here note," and Jupiter handed me a note which ran thus:

> My dear ——,
>   I have something to tell you, yet hardly know how to tell it, or whether I should tell it at all. If you can spare the time, come over with Jupiter. *Do* come. I wish to see you *tonight* on very grave business. Ever yours,
>
> William Legrand

Something in the tone of the note made me very uneasy. I feared that the loss of his fortune had at last unsettled his mind. I got ready at once to go back with Jupiter.

Upon reaching the wharf, I saw a sickle and three spades, all new, lying in the bottom of the boat which was to carry us across to the island.

"What are the tools for, Jupiter?" I asked.

"Them is what Master Will told me to buy for him."

"What is he going to do with a sickle and three spades?"

"That is more than I know, and devil take me if I don't believe it's more than he know, too. But it all comes of the bug."

Finding I could learn little from Jupiter, whose thought seemed entirely taken up with "the bug," I stepped into the boat, and made sail. With a fair and strong breeze, we soon ran into the little cove to the northward of Fort Moultrie, and a walk of some two miles brought us to the hut, about three in the afternoon.

Legrand met me and grasped my hand with an eager force that gave me added worry about his mental health. His face was very pale, and his deep-set eyes glowed with more than usual brightness.

I asked him, for sake of something to say, whether he had got back the beetle from Lieutenant G——.

"Oh, yes," he said, his face flushing. "Jupiter was right in calling it a bug of *real gold.*" He said this very seriously, and I felt a deep shock.

"Luck has given it to me," he went on with a smile. "I have only to use it right and I shall again be a man of fortune. Jupiter, bring me that beetle!"

"What! The bug, master? I'd rather not trouble that bug—you must get him for your own self."

Legrand rose and brought me the beetle from a glass case. It was beautiful—two round black spots near one end of the back and a long one near the other end. The scales, very hard and glossy, looked like polished gold. It was strangely heavy. I could hardly blame Jupiter for thinking it was gold. But why Legrand should think so, I could not, for the life of me, tell.

"I sent for you," he said, "to get your advice and help in carrying out the views of fate and of the bug—"

"My dear Legrand," I said, "you are unwell. You shall to to bed, and I will stay with you a few days, until you get over this fever—"

"Feel my pulse," he said.

I felt it, and found no sign of fever.

"I am as well," he said, " as I can expect to be under the strain that I bear. If you really wish me well, you will help me get rid of the strain."

"And how is this to be done?"

"Very easily. Jupiter and I are going up into the hills, on the mainland. We need the help of a third person. You are the only one we can trust. Whether we win or fail in what we go for, the strain will be lifted."

"I should like to help you, in any way," I said. "But does this infernal beetle have anything to do with your trip into the hills on the mainland?"

"It has."

"Then, Legrand, I will take part in no such foolish affair."

"I am sorry—very sorry—we must try it by ourselves, then."

The man is surely mad, I thought. "Not by yourselves," I said. "How long do you expect to be gone?"

"Probably all night. We start at once, and should be back at least by sunrise."

"Will you promise me that when this freak of yours is over—and the bug business settled—that you will come home and take my advice as if I were your doctor?"

"Yes, I promise. Now let us be off, for we have no time to lose."

With a heavy heart I went with him. We started about four o'clock—Legrand, Jupiter, the dog, and myself. Jupiter had with him the sickle and three spades. He *would* carry all of them himself, it seemed to me for fear they might otherwise come into the hands of his master. Jupiter's manner was dogged, and "that bug!" were the only words he spoke during the journey. I carried a couple of lanterns, and Legrand was left free-handed, except for the beetle, which he carried by a string tied to it, whirling it to and fro as he went.

My heart was heavy with pity to see in my friend's manner such signs of a wandering mind. I humored his fancy, but tried by roundabout questions to learn where we were going and why. But he was unwilling to talk, and to all my questions would say only, "We shall see!"

We crossed the creek, leaving the island, and started up the high shores of the mainland, going through a wild, lonely country. Legrand led briskly ahead, as if he knew his way. He paused now and then to look for what seemed to be landmarks which he had learned when going over the ground before.

In this manner we traveled for about two hours. The sun was just setting when we came to a kind of tableland, in a region more dreary than any yet seen. It lay near the top of a steep hill, which was thickly wooded, gashed by ravines, and cluttered with huge boulders.

The tableland to which we had scrambled was overgrown thickly with brush. We soon saw we could not force a way through without the sickle. Legrand told Jupiter where to cut a path. It brought us to the foot of a very tall tulip tree. About it stood some eight or ten great oaks, but the tulip tree went far beyond them—and any other tree I ever saw—in the general majesty of its size and form.

When we reached this tree, Legrand turned to Jupiter, and asked him if he thought he could climb it. The old man seemed a little staggered by the question, and for some moments made no reply. At last, he went up to the huge trunk, walked slowly around it, looking at it carefully. Then he merely said:

"Yes, master, Jup can climb any tree he ever see in he life."

"Then up with you as soon as possible, for it will soon be too dark to see what we are about."

"How far mus' I go up, master?"

"Get up the main trunk first, and then I will tell you which way to go—and here—stop! take this beetle with you."

"The bug, Master Will!—the gold bug!" cried the man, drawing back in fear. "What for must I tote the bug 'way up the tree? Darned if I do!"

"If you are afraid, Jup, a great big man like you, to take hold of a little dead beetle, you can carry it up by the string. But if you do not take it up with you in some way, I shall have to break your head with this spade."

"*Me* feared the bug!" said Jupiter, shamed into obeying. "What I care for the bug?"

He took hold of the end of the string, and held it as far from him as he could. Then, gripping the huge tree trunk with his arms and knees, he wriggled himself into the first great fork.

"Which way mus' I go now, Master Will?" he called.

"Go up the largest branch—the one on this side," said Legrand.

Jupiter climbed until he was out of sight among the leaves. Soon his voice was heard in a sort of halloo, "How much fudder is I got to go?"

"How high up are you?" asked Legrand.

"Ever so far. Can see the sky out the top of the tree."

"Never mind the sky, but listen to what I say. Look down the trunk and count the limbs below on this side. How many limbs have you passed?"

"One, two, tree, four, five—I done pass five big limb, master, on this side."

"Then go one limb higher."

In a few minutes he called down that he had reached the seventh limb.

"Now, Jup," cried Legrand, seeming much excited, "I want you to work your way out upon that limb as far as you can. If you see anything strange, let me know."

By this time I had lost what little hope I had of my poor friend's sanity. I became seriously worried about getting him home. While I was thinking what was best to be done, Jupiter's voice was again heard.

" 'Most feared for to venture on this limb very far—it's dead limb pretty much all the way."

"Did you say it was a *dead* limb, Jupiter?" cried Legrand in a shaking voice.

"Yes, master, dead as a door nail."

"What in the name of heaven shall I do?" cried Legrand, as if in great distress.

"Do!" said I, glad of a chance to get in a word. "Why, come home and go to bed. Come now!—it's getting late, and you remember your promise."

"Jupiter," he cried, without noticing me in the least, "do you hear me?"

"Yes, Master Will, hear you ever so plain."

"Try the wood with your knife, and see if you think it very rotten."

"Him rotten, master," said the negro, in a few moments, "but might venture out a little way by *myself.*"

"By yourself! What do you mean?"

"I mean the bug. Suppose I drop him down?"

"As sure as you let that beetle fall, I will break your neck. Look here, Jupiter, do you hear me?"

"Yes, master. No need holler at me that way."

"Well! Now listen! If you will venture out on the limb as far as you think safe, and not let go of the beetle, I'll give you a silver dollar as soon as you get down."

"'Most out to the end now," said Jupiter.

"Out to the end!" Legrand fairly screamed. "Do you say you are out to the end of that limb?"

"Soon be to the end, master—o-o-o-o-oh! Lor-gol-a-mercy! What *is* this here on de tree?"

"Well!" cried Legrand joyfully, "what is it?"

"A skull—somebody left his head up the tree and the crows done gobble the meat off."

"A skull, you say! How is it fastened to the limb?"

"A great big nail in the skull."

"Now, Jupiter, do just as I tell you—do you hear?"

"Yes, master."

"Listen, then! Find the left eye of the skull."

"There ain't no eye left at all—crows done got 'em."

"Curse your foolishness! Do you know your right hand from your left?"

"Yes—my left hand is what I chops the wood with."

"To be sure—you are left-handed. And your left eye is on the same side as your left hand. Now find the left eye of the skull, or the place where the left eye has been. Have you found it?"

Here was a long pause. At length Jupiter said: "I got the left eye now—what mus' I do with it?"

"Let the beetle drop through it, as far as the string will reach—but be careful and not let go your hold of the string."

"All that done, Master Will. Look out for the bug there below!"

All this while Jupiter's body could not be seen for the leaves, but the beetle now dropped below the lowest leaves. It hung there, shining like gold in the last rays of the setting sun. If let go, it would have fallen at our feet. Legrand took the sickle and cleared a space three or four yards across, in the spot where we stood. He then told Jupiter to let go the string, and come down from the tree.

The beetle fell to the ground, and at the spot where it lay, Legrand drove a peg into the ground. Then he took from his pocket a tape measure, and fastened one end of it to the side of the tree trunk nearest the peg. Now he unrolled the tape until it reached the peg, and thence further unrolled it in the line set up by the two points of the tree and the peg for a distance of fifty feet. Here he drove a second peg, and about it cleared a circle four feet across. Then, taking up a spade, and giving one to Jupiter and one to me, he begged us to join him at once in digging.

To speak the truth, I had no will to dig, for I was weary with the journey, and night was coming on. But I would not go against Legrand's wishes, for fear of bringing on some outburst. If I could have been sure of Jupiter's aid, I would have tried to force Legrand to start home. But I knew the old servant too well to hope that he would obey me against his master's will. I did not doubt that Legrand's wandering mind had siezed on the idea of buried money, a fancy brought on perhaps by the finding the beetle which Jupiter had called a gold bug.

Sadly vexed and puzzled, I began to dig with a good will. Perhaps failure to find buried money would the sooner rouse Legrand from his fancy. The lanterns having been lit, we all went on with the work. As the glare fell upon us and our spades, I thought how strange we would look to anyone chancing to see us.

We dug very steadily for two hours. Little was said. The dog took great interest in our digging, and his yelping became so loud that Legrand feared some stragglers might be led to the spot. For myself, I should have been glad to see anyone who could help me get the wanderer home.

At the end of two hours, we were five feet deep. Legrand paused, and I began to hope this folly was at an end. But he only wiped his brow sadly, and began again. We had dug the pit four feet across, and now we made it some wider, and went down two feet further. Then the gold-seeker, whom I greatly pitied, climbed from the hole, bitter failure showing in his face. He went slowly and put on his coat. I waited, saying nothing. Jupiter, at a sign from his master, gathered up the tools, and we started, still silent, toward home.

We had gone about a dozen steps when Legrand, with a loud oath, turned and seized Jupiter by the collar. The servant opened wide his eyes and mouth, dropped the tools, and fell to his knees.

"You scoundrel!" said Legrand, hissing the words between clenched teeth. "Speak, I tell you! Which—which is your left eye?"

"Oh, my golly, Master Will! Ain't this here my left eye?" roared the terrified Jupiter, placing his hand upon his *right* eye, and holding it there as if he feared his master might gouge it out.

"I thought so! I knew it! Hurrah!" cried Legrand, letting him go, and dancing about in joy. "Come—we must go back—the game is not up yet!" And he led the way back toward the tulip tree.

"Jupiter," he said, when we reached its foot, "come here! Was the skull nailed to the limb with face outward, or with face to the limb?"

"The face was out, master, so that the crows could get at the eyes good."

"Well, then, was it this eye or that one, which you dropped the beetle through?" As Legrand spoke he touched Jupiter's eyes, one after the other.

"This eye, massa—the left eye—just as you tell me," and here the man again touched his *right* eye.

"That will do—we must try again."

Legrand—in whose madness I now saw some faint signs of method—moved the peg which marked the spot where the beetle fell, to a spot about three inches westward. Then, starting the tape measure at the point of the trunk, nearest the peg, he measured to the peg, and thence fifty feet further. At this spot we again cleared a circle, somewhat larger than the other, and set to work with the spades.

I was dreadfully weary, but now I had become interested in the work, even excited, and I dug eagerly. After we had been at work for perhaps an hour and a half, we were again troubled by the howlings of the dog. His yelping before had seemed to be caused by playful excitement. Now his howls sounded like a bitter wail. At last Jupiter climbed doggedly out of the pit to try to muzzle him. The dog sprang away from him, leaped into the pit, and began to tear the earth wildly with his claws. In a few seconds, he had uncovered a number of human bones, the remains of two human skeletons.

A few minutes later, a spade turned up the blade of a large Spanish knife. As we dug further, three or four loose pieces of gold and silver coin came to light. Jupiter, almost overcome with joy, gathered up the coins, but Legrand looked sadly disappointed. He urged us, however, to go on digging. Suddenly I stumbled and fell forward, having caught my toe in a large ring of iron that lay half buried in the earth.

We now worked in earnest, and never did I pass ten minutes of greater excitement. We soon uncovered a wooden chest three and a half feet long, three feet broad, and two and a half feet deep, firmly held by bands of iron forming a kind of trelliswork over the whole. It was heavier than we could lift. Luckily it was fastened only by two sliding bolts. These we drew back—and a treasure of countless value lay gleaming before us.

The rays of the lantern fell on a mixed heap of gold and

jewels that flashed and glowed to dazzle our eyes. What I felt was chiefly the shock of surprise. Legrand was limp with excitement and spoke very few words. Jupiter was thunderstruck, his face as pale as it could become. He kneeled and buried his arms up to the elbows in gold, as if enjoying a bath.

"And this is all come of the gold bug," he said, with a deep sigh. "De pretty gold bug! De pore little gold bug what I talked so mean about. Ain't you 'shamed of yourself, Jup—answer me dat."

It was growing late, and we must get the treasure housed before daylight. So shocked as we were, it was some time before we could hit upon a plan. Finally we lightened the box by taking out two-thirds of the treasure, and then raised it from the pit. We hid part of the treasure among the bushes, and left the dog to guard it, with strict orders from Jupiter not to stir from the spot nor open his mouth until we returned. We then hurriedly made for home with the chest. We reached the hut, after great toil, at one o'clock in the morning. Worn out as we were, we could not do more, but had supper and rested until two o'clock.

Soon after, we started for the hills, taking three sturdy sacks. A little before four o'clock we reached the pit. We divided the rest of the treasure among us, and leaving the hole unfilled, set out again for the hut, which we reached about dawn. We were now thoroughly tired. After a sleep of three or four hours, we arose and spent the rest of the day going over and sorting the treasure.

In coin, there was rather more than $450,000. There was no silver. All was gold of old date and many kinds—French, Spanish, German, English, and some coins the like of which we had never seen before. There was no American money. The value of the jewels we could hardly guess at. There were diamonds—some of them very large and fine—100 in all. There were 18 rubies of great beauty; 310 emeralds, all very fine; 22 sapphires; and one opal. The stones had all been taken from their settings and thrown loose in the chest. The settings themselves we picked out from among the other gold.

Besides all this, there was a great amount of solid gold; nearly 200 massive ear and finger rings; rich chains, 30 of these, if I remember; 83 very large and heavy crosses; five gold censers of great value; a huge golden punch bowl, beautifully engraved with vine leaves and dancing figures; two sword handles, richly made, and many other smaller articles.

Besides all this, there were 197 gold watches, three of them worth at least $500 apiece. As timekeepers they had no value—but they were in cases of great value, richly set with jewels.

We judged the entire treasure at a million and a half dollars. But later, when we sold the trinkets and jewels (keeping a few for our own use), we found that we had greatly undervalued the treasure.

Later, when our excitement had somewhat passed, Legrand told me how he had been led to find the treasure.

"You remember," he said, "the night that I made you a rough drawing of the beetle. You may have noticed that I became vexed when you said the drawing looked like a death's-head, for I believe myself to be a fairly good artist. When you handed me back the scrap of parchment—"[3]

"You mean the scrap of paper," I said.

"No. It looked like paper, but when I came to draw upon it, I saw it was a piece of very thin parchment, quite dirty. Well, you handed back the scrap of parchment, and I was about to crumple it up, when I saw on it the death's-head that you had been looking at. I was too much surprised to think clearly. I knew that I had not drawn a death's-head, though my drawing had a certain likeness to one, in outline. Turning the parchment over, I saw my drawing of the beetle, on the other side.

[3]The skin of a sheep, goat, or other animal, prepared for writing purposes.

"Now, there had been *no* death's-head on the parchment when I made my sketch of the beetle. I was certain of this, for I remembered turning it over in search of the cleanest spot. Had the death's-head been there then, of course I would have seen it. The moment I saw the death's-head, I felt a faint glimmer of the truth, but I put the parchment away until I should be alone.

"When you had gone and Jupiter was asleep, I set myself to think through the matter. First I recalled where I had got the parchment. We had found the beetle on the coast of the mainland, a short distance above high-water mark. It had bitten me when I took hold of it, causing me to let it drop. Looking about for a leaf or something of the kind, by which to take hold of it, we found what looked like a scrap of paper lying half-buried in the sand, a corner sticking up. With this, Jupiter picked up the beetle.

"On the way home, we met Lieutenant G——. I showed him the beetle, and he asked to take it to the fort. I agreed, and he put it into his pocket. I had been holding the parchment as he looked at the insect, and now instead of throwing it down, I thrust it into my pocket, purely by habit, without thought.

"When you handed back the parchment, and I saw the death's-head on it, I first put together two links of a chain. I remembered seeing the remains of a wrecked boat near where we found the parchment. The skull, or death's-head, is the well-known emblem of pirates. They run up the death's-head flag in all sea fights."

"But," I broke in, "you said that the skull was *not* on the parchment when you made the drawing of the beetle."

"Ah, here turns the whole mystery. You know, of course, that by using certain chemicals for ink, we can make a writing which will fade away after some time, but will again appear when the paper is heated. You will remember that when I gave you the drawing made on the parchment, you were sitting by a blazing fire. And just as you were in the act

of looking at the drawing, the dog was let in, and he leaped upon you. With your left hand, you stroked him and pushed him off, while your right hand, holding the parchment, rested on your knee, close to the blazing fire—so close that one moment I feared it might catch fire.

"When I thought of all this, I knew that the *heat* had made the death's-head come to light. I saw that some of the lines were not clear. I held the parchment close to a glowing heat, and there came into view in the lower right-hand corner, a crude drawing of a goat or a kid. Everyone has heard of Captain Kidd,[4] the pirate. 'This,' I said to myself, 'is the picture of a kid. Standing in the lower right-hand corner, it is a kind of picture-signature.'

"You have heard some of the many stories about money

[4] A famous pirate hanged in London in 1701.

The Gold Bug

being buried somewhere on the Atlantic coast, by Captain Kidd. That he had a great store of treasure is well known. In short, I was almost certain that the parchment was a lost record of where treasure was buried."

"But how did you know where to look for it?"

"I will tell you. I held the parchment still closer to the fire, but nothing more showed on it. Then I cleaned away the dirt from the parchment by pouring warm water over it. Next I placed it in a tin pan, with the drawings downward, and set the pan on lighted coals. In a few minutes, it had become thoroughly heated. I looked at it again, and to my joy found it spotted with figures written in lines. I put it back in the pan and left it there for another minute. On taking it out, the whole was just as you see it now."

Here Legrand, having reheated the parchment, handed it to me. The following marks, rudely traced in a red tint, were between the death's-head and the goat:

53‡‡†305))6*;4826)4‡.)4‡);806*;48†8¶60))85;;]8*;:‡*
8†83(88)5*†;46(;88*96*?;8)*‡(;485);5*†2:*‡(;4956*2(5*
—4)8¶8*;4069285);)6†8)4‡‡;1(‡9;48081;8:8‡1;48†85;4)48
5†528806*81(‡9;48;(88;4(‡?34;48)4‡161;:188;‡?;

"But," I said, "I am as much in the dark as ever."

"It is a secret writing, or code; but not so hard to read as you might think. From what is known of Kidd, I believed the secret writing was one of the simpler kinds, though the mind of the crude sailor would think that no one could solve it without a key."

"And you really solved it?"

"Easily. I have solved others ten times harder. I have always been interested in such riddles. In fact, I doubt that human cunning can set up a code which human cunning cannot solve."

"And how did you go about solving this one?"

"The first question in solving any secret writing is, What is the *language* of the writing? Generally, one must learn this by trying out every language known to him, until the right one is found. In this case, I was spared the trouble. The pun on the word *kid* points only to the English language.

"You notice there are no spaces between words. Had there been, the task would have been very easy. I should have begun with the shorter words, certainly with words of a single letter—*a* or *I*. But as there were no spaces, my first step was to make a table of how often each figure appeared in the code."

Legrand handed me the following table:

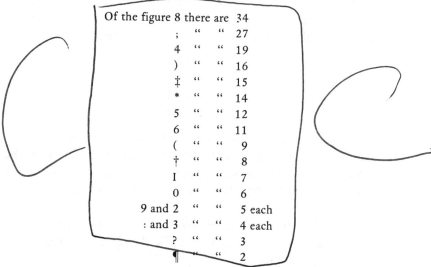

Of the figure 8 there are			34
;	"	"	27
4	"	"	19
)	"	"	16
‡	"	"	15
*	"	"	14
5	"	"	12
6	"	"	11
(	"	"	9
†	"	"	8
I	"	"	7
0	"	"	6
9 and 2	"	"	5 each
: and 3	"	"	4 each
?	"	"	3
¶	"	"	2

"Now, in English, the letter used most often is *e*. Looking at the table, we see that the figure 8 appears most often—34 times. We will say that 8 stands for *e*. We notice, too, that 8 is seen often in couples, and we know that *e* is often doubled in English words: *meet, fleet, speed, seen, been, agree*, etc.

"Next, to find a word. Of all words in the language, the one most used is *the*. Let us look, therefore, for three figures in the same order—last one being 8—which appear grouped thus more than once. We find the following group appearing seven times: ;48. If we say this group of figures is *the,* the semicolon stands for *t,* the 4 for *h,* and of course the 8 for *e.*

"If the group is *the,* the first figure following it is the first letter in another word. See, at center of this last long line of the code, a group of ;48. Beginning at this point, let us set under the figures the letters, leaving a blank for the unknown, thus:

   ; 4 8   ; (8 8   ; 4 (‡ ? 3 4   ; 4 8 etc.
   t h e t   e e t h

Here we stop and search for a letter to fill the blank. By going through the entire alphabet, letter by letter, we see that the only letters that can be used between *t* and *ee* are

        t *h* eeth
        t *l* eeth
        t *r* eeth
        t *w* eeth

But these are not English words. We now know that no *word* can be formed which will take in the final *th.* We drop the final *th,* and two words appear—*thee* and *tree. The thee* makes no sense, but *the tree* does. Thus we gain another letter, *r.*

"Looking beyond these words, for a short distance, we see another group of ;48, and fill the space between with known letters, thus:

   ; 4 8 ; (8 8 ; 4 (‡ ? 3 4 ; 4 8 etc.
   t h e t r e e t h r   h t h e

The unfinished word is plainly *through,* and we have three new letters, *o, u, g.*

"Going to the beginning of the code, we find

        5 3 ‡ ‡ † etc.
        g o o

Thus we have what seems to be the beginning of *good,*

and the single figure before the word can be only *a—a good.*
We have added two more to the known letters, *a* and *d.*

"It is now time to arrange our key, or the table of letters
so far learned, thus:

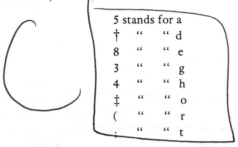

5 stands for	a
† " "	d
8 " "	e
3 " "	g
4 " "	h
‡ " "	o
(" "	r
; " "	t

Here we have, already, eight of the most used letters. We
need not go further into the method. You can see that the
code is very simple, since the key to it can be thus easily
found. Without troubling you longer with the code, I will
give you the words spelled out by the figures on the parchment. Here they are." He handed me a paper on which he
had written:

A good glass in the bishop's hostel in the devil's
seat twenty-one degrees and thirteen minutes
northeast and by north main branch seventh limb
east side shoot from the left eye of the death's-
head a beeline from the tree through the shot
fifty feet out.

"But," I said, "I am as much at a loss as ever. How did
you get any meaning out of *devil's seat* and *bishop's hostel?*"

"My first task was to divide the sentences into phrases. I
divided it thus."

Legrand then separated the words on the sheet so that
they appeared:

A good glass in the bishop's hostel in the devil's
seat—twenty-one degrees and thirteen minutes—

23

northeast and by north—main branch seventh limb east side—shoot from the left eye of the death's-head—a beeline from the tree through the shot fifty feet out.

"Even this," I said, "leaves me still in the dark."

"It left me also in the dark," replied Legrand. "I asked people around Sullivan's Island for any building that went by the name of Bishop's hotel—for of course I dropped the old word *hostel.* But I could learn nothing on the subject. Then it came into my head quite suddenly that by *Bishop* was meant the name of an old family called Bessop, which time out of mind has owned a plantation about four miles northward of the island. I went over to the plantation and inquired among the older servants, about the place. An old black woman said that she had heard of a Bessop's castle, but that it was not a castle nor a hotel, but a large rock. I paid her to direct me there, which she easily did.

"I found that the so-called castle was a very high rock. I climbed to the top. Looking around me, I saw a narrow ledge or shelf on the eastern face of the rock about a yard below where I stood. It was about eighteen inches by twelve, and a hollow in the rock just above the ledge made the whole look like one of those hollow-backed chairs used by our ancestors. I made no doubt that here was the *devil's seat.* And now I seemed to grasp the full secret of the riddle.

"The good glass would be a telescope. Sailors almost always speak of a telescope as a *glass.* No doubt, too, the *twenty-one degrees and thirteen minutes,* and *northeast* and *by north* were directions for leveling the glass. Greatly excited, I hurried home for a telescope, and returned to the rock.

"I climbed down to the ledge, and found I could sit on it in only one position. I was now ready to level the glass. Of course the *twenty-one degrees and thirteen minutes* named the elevation above the horizon; and the *northeast and by*

north named the direction on the horizon. I soon found the horizontal direction by means of a compass. Then pointing the glass as nearly at an angle of twenty-one degrees elevation as I could guess, I moved it slowly about until I noticed an opening in the leaves of a large tree that overtopped all others in the distance. In this opening I saw a white spot, which at last I made out to be a skull. The puzzle was now solved."

"I suppose," I said, "that Kidd used the skull's eye to let fall a weight through, because the death's-head is on the pirate's flag."

"Perhaps so. But common sense may have caused him to use it. To be seen so far, a small object must be white. There is nothing like your human skull to grow whiter and whiter in all weather."

"But why did you let fall the beetle through the skull, instead of a bullet or other small weight? I was sure you were mad."

"Why, to be frank, I was vexed because you *did* think so, and wished to punish you quietly by a little bit of mystery. Then, too, the beetle's weight made it useful for the purpose."

"What are we to make of the two skeletons found in the pit?"

"It is likely that Kidd—if Kidd indeed buried the treasure—would wish to keep the hiding place secret from everyone. Yet, it is clear that he must have had help to carry and bury the treasure there. So, when the heaviest of the labor was done, he may have killed those who helped him. Perhaps a couple of blows with a spade were enough, while the workers were busy in the pit. Perhaps it took a dozen blows—who can tell?"

The Murders in the Rue Morgue

My friend Auguste Dupin was fond of puzzles, riddles, secret writings, and liked to unravel any problem. He and I shared an apartment in Paris, and I often saw him working on some question. The ease and speed with which he found the answer always caused me to look on him with wonder.

Dupin was a modest man, and made no boast of his great mental powers. But one day he said to me, with a low chuckle, that most men wore on their chests a window open to his eyes, if he cared to pry within.

One evening I was looking over the day's newspaper, when I saw the following:

TWO WOMEN MURDERED—This morning about three o'clock, people of the Rue[1] Morgue were roused by loud screams coming from the home of Madame L'Espanaye and her daughter, Camille. Several people ran to the place, but the door was locked. By the time police officers reached the house, and broke open the door, the cries had ceased. They heard angry voices coming from the upper floor, but by the time they had reached the second floor, these sounds too had ceased.

The entering party hurried from room to room. The door to a back room on the fourth floor was locked with the key

[1] French for street.

inside. When the door was forced open, they found the furniture broken and thrown about, and the bedding torn from the bed and lying on the floor. On a chair was a razor smeared with blood. On the hearth were tresses of gray human hair, pulled out by the roots, and dabbled in blood. On the floor were found some coins, a topaz earring, three large silver spoons, three smaller ones, and two bags holding nearly four thousand francs in gold. The drawers of a bureau were open, and seemingly had been rifled, though many articles were left in them. A small iron safe was found under the bedding on the floor. The safe was open, with the key still in the door. It held only a few old letters and other papers of little value.

Nothing was seen of Madame L'Espanaye or her daughter. But a large amount of soot was lying in the fireplace, and they soon found the corpse of the daughter thrust up the chimney, head downward. It had been forced up the narrow throat of the chimney for some distance, and showed many bruises and scratches, which could have been caused by being thrust up, or dragged from the narrow chimney. Upon the throat were dark bruises, showing that the victim had been strangled to death.

In a small paved yard behind the building, the corpse of Madame L'Espanaye was found. Her throat had been cut so deeply that when the body was raised, the head fell off. The body, as well as the head, was fearfully bruised.

The newspaper story ended thus: To this horrible murder there is not as yet the least clue.

Next day's newspaper gave a report of what police had learned from persons who had been questioned about the murder.

Pauline Dubourg states that she has known Madame L'Espanaye and her daughter for three years, having washed for them during that time. They paid well. Knew nothing of

their means of living, but believed Madame L'Espanaye told fortunes for a living. Had heard that she had money saved. Never met any person in the house when she called for the clothes or took them home. Was sure they had no servant.

Pierre Moreau states that he was born in that street and has always lived there. Madame L'Espanaye had long owned the house she lived in. The house was once rented to a jeweler, who rented the upper rooms to others. Madame L'Espanaye thought the tenants were not taking care of the house. Six years ago she moved into it herself, and would not rent any part of it. The old lady was childish. Witness had seen the daughter some five or six times during the six years they had lived there. The two lived a very quiet life, but were said to have money. Had heard it said that Madame L'Espanaye told fortunes—did not believe it. Had never seen anyone enter the door but the old lady and her daughter, a porter once or twice, and a doctor a few times.

Other witnesses told about the same story. They had seen no one visit the house. They did not know whether the two women had any living relatives. The front window shutters were seldom opened. Those in the rear were always closed, except those of the large back room, fourth story, where the two lived.

Isidore Muset, police officer, states that he was called to the house about three o'clock in the morning. Found several people already there, trying to get in. Had little trouble forcing the door open, it being a double or folding door, and bolted neither at bottom or top. The screams had stopped about the time the door was forced open. They seemed to come from someone in great agony—were loud and drawn out, not short and quick. Upon reaching the first landing, heard two voices, loud and angry—one a gruff voice, the other shrill, a very strange voice. Could understand some words of the gruff voice, which were in French. Was sure it was not a woman's voice. Had understood the words *sacré* and *diable.*[2] The shrill voice was that of a foreigner. Could not be sure whether it was the voice of a man or a woman. Believed the language was Spanish.

Henri Duval states that he was one of the party who first entered the house. Agrees with Muset in general. Thinks the shrill voice was that of an Italian. Was certain it was not French. Could not be sure that it was a man's voice. It might have been a woman's. Does not know the Italian language. Had talked with Madame L'Espanaye and her daughter often. Was sure the shrill voice was not that of either.

— — *Odenheimer,* restaurant keeper. This man volunteered to testify. Since he could not speak French, he was examined through an interpreter. Said he is a native of Amsterdam. Was passing the house at the time of the screams. They lasted about ten minutes, long and loud, very fearful to hear. He was one who entered the building. Agreed with other

[2] Damned and devil.

witnesses in every matter but one. Was sure that the shrill voice was a Frenchman's. Could not understand the words. They were loud and quick—spoken it seemed in fear and anger. The voice was not so much shrill as harsh. Could not call it a shrill voice.

Jules Mignaud, banker, states that Madame L'Espanaye had some property. Had opened an account with his bank eight years ago. Often brought in small sums to deposit. Had withdrawn nothing until the third day before her death, when she took out, in person, the sum of four thousand francs. This sum the bank paid in gold, and sent a clerk home with her, to guard the money.

Adolphe Le Bon, bank clerk, states that he went with Madame L'Espanaye to her home with the four thousand francs, which he carried in two bags. The daughter opened the door to them and took one of the bags from his hand, while Madame L'Espanaye took the other. He then left. Did not see anyone in the street at the time. It is a by-street, very lonely.

William Bird, tailor, states that he was one of the party that entered the house. Is an Englishman, and has lived in Paris two years. Was one of the first to run up the stairs. Heard the angry voices. The gruff voice was that of a Frenchman. Could make out several words, but cannot now remember all. Clearly heard the words *sacré* and *mon Dieu.*[3] Heard sound as if persons were struggling within—scraping, scuffling sounds. The shrill voice was very loud—louder than the gruff one. Is sure it was not the voice of an Englishman. Sounded like a German. Might have been a woman's voice. He does not understand German.

Alfonzo Garcio, undertaker, states that he lives in the Rue Morgue. Is a native of Spain. Was one of the party who entered the house. Did not go up the stairs, because he is nervous. Heard the voices. The gruff voice was that of a

[3] My God.

31

Frenchman. Could not understand what was said. The shrill voice was that of an Englishman—is sure of this. Does not understand English, but judged by the tones.

Alberto Montani, shopkeeper, states that he was among the first to go up the stairs. Agrees in general with the other witnesses. States that the gruff voice was that of a Frenchman. Understood several words. Could not make out the words of the shrill voice. Thinks it the voice of a Russian. He himself is Italian. He never talked with a native of Russia.

Paul Dumas, doctor, states that he was called to view the bodies about daybreak. The corpse of the young woman was much bruised and scratched. The fact that it had been thrust up the narrow chimney would account for this. There were several deep scratches just below the chin, and a number of bruises seemingly made by fingers. A large bruise in the pit of the stomach could have been made by pressure of a knee. The face was fearfully discolored, the eyeballs protruded, and the tongue was partly bitten through. In his opinion, the young woman had been strangled to death. The corpse of the mother was horribly broken. All bones of the right leg and arm were more or less shattered. The left tibia[4] was splintered, as well as all the ribs of the left side. Any large, blunt weapon—a heavy club of wood—a broad bar of iron—a chair—could have caused such injuries in the hands of a powerful man. No woman would be strong enough to give such blows with any weapon. The throat had been cut with a sharp tool—probably a razor.

Four of the above named witnesses, being recalled, stated that the door of the room in which was found the body of the daughter Camille was locked with the key inside. By the time they had reached the door, all was silent. They heard no groans or noises of any kind. Upon forcing the door, they saw no person in the room. The windows were down and firmly fastened from within. The time it took to break open

---

[4] One of the long bones in the lower part of the leg.

the door to the back room was said by some to be three *C* minutes, by others to be five. A small room in the front of the house, at the head of the stairs was open, the door being ajar. This room was crowded with old beds, boxes, and so forth. These were carefully removed and searched. A trap door on the roof was nailed down—did not appear to have been opened for years.

Several witnesses, when recalled, stated that the chimneys of all the rooms on the fourth floor are too narrow to allow a human body to pass through. There is no back way by which anyone could have gone down, while the party was coming up the front stairs.

The newspaper story ended by saying: "Nothing further has been learned of this brutal murder. The police are at a loss. There is not the shadow of a clue to explain the mystery."

The evening paper stated that Adolphe Le Bon had been arrested, though nothing new had been learned of the crime.

Dupin had seemed greatly interested in this case. But it was not until he read of Le Bon's arrest that he asked me what I thought of the case.

"What do I think? I can merely agree with the newspapers—there seems to be no clue."

"Paris police are cunning, but not deep," said Dupin. "As for these murders, let us make a search ourselves. It will amuse us, and besides, Le Bon once did me a favor, for which I am grateful. Come, we will go see the house with our own eyes. I know the Prefect of Police, and he will let us enter."

It was late in the afternoon when we reached the place. It was easily found, for several persons stood gazing up at the closed shutters, in idle curiosity. Before going in, we walked up the street, turned down an alley, and passed in the rear of the building. Dupin all the while looked about him with a care that I could see no reason for.

We went around to the front of the house again, rang, and having shown our card to the officer in charge, were

ed to enter. We went upstairs—into the room where the
of Camille L'Espanaye had been found, and where the
bodies of both victims still lay.

Everything had been left as it was found. I saw nothing
beyond what had been printed in the newspapers. Dupin,
however, looked carefully at everything there—even at the
bodies. We then went into the other rooms, and into the
yard. It was dark when we finished our examination and left.
On the way home, Dupin stopped for a moment at the office
of one of the daily papers.

He said nothing about the murder until about noon the
next day. Then he suddenly asked me if I had noticed anything *strange* or *unusual* about the crime.

"No, nothing," I said. "At least nothing more than we
read in the papers."

"It seems," he said, "that the police cannot solve this
crime for the very reason that makes it easy to solve—I mean
its *strange* or *unusual* nature. The police are at a standstill
because they can find no motive for a murder so brutal.
That is unusual. They are puzzled, too, by the fact that although voices were heard in the room, there was no
way for a murderer to leave the room unseen. That, too,
is unusual. And so the police are blinded by the *unusual.* Yet
I shall solve the crime easily, and because of this very *unusual*
which has blinded the police."

I could only stare at Dupin in mute wonder.

"I am now awaiting," he said, looking toward the door
of our apartment, "a person who must have been connected
in some way with the crime. Of the worst part of the crime,
I believe he is not guilty. I hope so, for upon that idea I have
built my plan to solve the mystery. I look for the man
here—in this room—any moment. He may not come, but it
is likely that he will. If he comes, it will be our duty to hold
him. Here are pistols, and we both know how to use them
when need arises."

I took the pistols, hardly knowing what I did, or understanding what I heard. Dupin went on speaking, almost as if thinking aloud. He spoke in an absent-minded way, his eyes vacant, fixed only on the wall. This was his usual manner when at work on some knotty problem.

"That the voices heard in the room," he said, "were not the voices of the women was fully proved by the witnesses. This does away with any idea that the old lady could have first killed the daughter and afterward herself. Besides, she would not have been strong enough to thrust her daughter's body up the chimney. Moreover, her own death wound was one that she could not have made herself. The murder, then, was done by some third party, and the voice of this third party was one of those heard. Did you notice anything strange about what the witnesses said of these voices?"

"They all agreed that the gruff voice was that of a Frenchman. But they did not agree as to the shrill, or—as one called it—the harsh voice."

"True," said Dupin. "But you did not notice that all agreed that the shrill voice was the voice of a foreigner, but they could not agree on what language was spoken. One Frenchman thought it was the voice of a Spaniard, and that he might have understood some words, *if he had known Spanish*. The German thought it was the voice of a Frenchman, but he himself *does not understand French*. The Englishman thought it the voice of a German, and *does not understand German*. The Spaniard was sure it was the voice of an Englishman, but *he judged by the tone, for he has no knowledge of English*. The Italian believed it was the voice of a Russian, but *has never talked with a native of Russia*. A second Frenchman differs from the first. He was sure the voice was that of an Italian, but *not knowing the Italian tongue, he judged by the tones*. And one witness said the voice was harsh rather than shrill."

"But what has this to do with solving the crime?"

"It was enough to direct my search for the murderer," said Dupin. "But, now, let us think of every possible way that the murderer might have left the room. The police have examined the walls and ceilings of the place, and say there is no secret door. But not trusting to their eyes, I searched with my own. There is *no* secret door, and the door leading into the hall was locked with the key inside. The chimney, beyond some eight or ten feet above the hearth, is too small to allow the body of a large cat to pass through.

"The police found that the two windows of the room were fastened from within by a stout nail that was fitted into a hole which went through the sash and into the frame. They found that the windows could not be raised by force. They did not, however, pull out the nail and open the windows, but left them as found. Now, I reasoned that the murderer *must* have passed out through one of those windows. I went to one, took out the nail, and tried to raise the sash. As I expected, it could not be done; a hidden spring was holding it, and search soon brought it to light. I saw that if a person passed out this window and closed it behind him, the spring would catch and fasten itself."

"Ah, but the nail could not be put back into the hole, by one outside the window!"

"That is true. But I was not for a moment at a loss. I knew that the murderer had left through the other window. I went to the other window, which was partly covered by the headboard of the bedstead. Here I saw the same kind of fastener, a stout nail fitted into a hole made in the left side of the sash. Reason told me that this *nail* was the key to the problem. It looked like the nail in the other window, but it *must* be different, for through this window the murderer must have passed. I got upon the bedstead, looked over and found the secret spring, like that on the other window. I now looked at the nail. It looked like the other nail—that is, pushed in nearly to the head. But when I pressed the secret spring, I was able to raise the sash—the nail went up with it. When I took hold of the nail to draw it out, the head with a very short piece of the shank came off in

my fingers. I closed the window, put back the broken nail, and there again was the window fastened tight, seemingly by the nail. Plainly the murderer had passed out through this window. When he was outside, the window had dropped, or been closed, and the secret spring had caught."

"Then this window was held by the spring, not by the nail, as the police thought."

"Yes. The next question was how the murderer got down from the fourth floor. This I had solved in my walk with you around the building. About five and a half feet from the window there runs a lightning rod, too far for one to reach from it to the window. But the upper half of the shutters are made of lattice work, giving good hand hold. These shutters are fully three and a half feet broad, and if swung wide, would be within two feet of the lightning rod. By very unusual activity and courage one might enter the window from the lightning rod, by means of catching onto the shutter. I wish you to keep in mind that I say a *very unusual* activity would be needed to do this. I wish you to think of this *very unusual* activity with that *very strange* shrill, or harsh voice, about which no two witnesses could agree.

"The bureau drawers, it is said, had been rifled. That was a mere guess—a very silly one. Nearly the whole of the four thousand francs was found, in bags, upon the floor. Why would a thief leave four thousand francs in gold and carry off a bundle of linens?

"Now let us glance at the murder itself. A woman strangled to death, and thrust up a chimney—head downward, an act contrary to human action. Think, too, what great strength was needed for this. The united force of several men was hardly great enough to drag it *down!*

"Think, too, of other signs of great strength. On the hearth were thick locks of gray human hair, torn out by the roots. You know what great force is needed to tear from the head even twenty or thirty hairs together. And the throat of the old lady was not merely cut—the head was almost separated from the body, by a mere razor. I wish you to think of the *brutal force* of these deeds. I do not speak of the bruises and broken bones of the body of Madame L'Espanaye. The police have said they were caused by some blunt weapon. But the blunt weapon was the stone pavement that the body struck when thrown from the window. The police did not think of this, because they believed no window had been opened.

"Now, you have these clues—no motive of robbery, the unusual activity needed to get into the room, the signs of a strength greater than human, the brutal acts unlike human action, and a voice foreign to men of many nations—what do you make of it?"

I felt a creeping of the flesh as Dupin asked me the question. "A madman," I said, "has committed this awful deed—some raving madman."

"But a madman's voice is like that of other men, and his words will be those of his native language. Also, look at this little tuft of tawny hair, which I took from the clenched fingers of Madame L'Espanaye. What do you make of it?"

"Dupin!" I cried, "this is not *human* hair."

"I have not said it is," he replied. "Now, here is a drawing, made to scale, of the bruises and fingernail marks upon the throat of the murdered young woman. You will see," he said, laying the paper on the table before us, "that the drawing shows a fixed grasp—there was no *slipping* of the fingers. Each finger has held the same fearful grip until the death of the victim. Try, now, to fit all your fingers at the same time, to the drawing."

I tried in vain.

"Perhaps we are not giving it a fair trial," he said. "The paper is flat. Let us bend it into a tube about the size of the human throat. Now try again."

I did so, but was even further from being able to fit my fingers to the drawing.

"This is not the mark of a human hand," I said.

"Read now this page," said Dupin, handing me a book.

It was a description of the large tawny orangutan of the East Indian islands. It told of the giant size, the great strength and activity, the wild fierceness of these apes, and the way they like to imitate. Now I understood the full horror of the murders.

"But," I said, "what about the voices that were heard?"

"One was the voice of a Frenchman, who saw the murders. It is likely that he took no hand in it. If so, this notice which I left last night at the office of this newspaper, will bring him here."

He handed me the day's copy of a paper which printed shipping news, and was much read by sailors. I read the notice:

CAUGHT—early in the morning of July 18 [the morning of the murders], a very large, tawny orangutan. The owner, who is known to be a sailor, may have the animal by proving owner-ship and paying for its capture and keep.

The notice ended by asking the owner to call at an address, which was that of our apartment.

"How could you know the man is a sailor?" I asked.

"I am not *sure* of it. But here is a piece of ribbon, which from its form and greasy look, could have been used to tie the hair in one of those *queues*[5] that sailors wear. I picked it up at the foot of the lightning rod. Now, if I am wrong in what I have guessed from this ribbon—that the Frenchman is a sailor—still I have done no harm in saying that he is a sailor. But if I am right, I have gained something. For, at first, the man will fear to claim the orangutan, lest he be accused of the murder. But later, he will reason thus: 'The police do not know who did the murders—And already it is known that the beast was owned by a sailor—it will be traced to me, and the police will want to know why I did not claim it—The safest thing is to claim it, and keep it close until the matter has blown over.' "

At this moment we heard a step on the stairs.

"Be ready," said Dupin, "with your pistols, but do not use or show them without a sign from me."

The front door of the house had been left open, and the visitor had entered without ringing. He now rapped at our door.

"Come in," said Dupin, in cheerful, hearty tone.

A man entered. He had the look of a sailor. He was tall, stout, muscular, with a sunburnt face half hidden by whiskers. He carried a huge oak club, but seemed otherwise without arms. He bowed awkwardly and said "Good evening."

[5] Braids of hair.

"Sit down, my friend," said Dupin. "You have called about the orangutan. A very fine and no doubt very valuable animal. How old do you think he is?"

The sailor drew a long breath, like one freed of a burden, and replied, "I have no way of telling—but he can't be more than four or five years old. Have you got him here?"

"Oh no. We had no way to keep him here. He is at a livery stable near by. You can claim him there. Of course you are ready to prove he is yours."

"To be sure, I am, sir. And I am willing to pay a reward—that is, anything in reason."

"That is fair," said Dupin. "Now let me think—what reward shall I ask? Oh, I will tell you. My reward shall be this: You shall tell me all you know about these murders in the Rue Morgue."

Dupin spoke the last words in a low tone, and very quietly. Just as quietly, too, he walked to the door, locked it, drew a pistol from his pocket, and placed it upon the table.

The sailor started to his feet and grasped his club, but

the next moment sat down again, his face pale as death. He spoke not a word. I pitied him from the bottom of my heart.

"My friend," said Dupin, in a kind tone, "I know very well that you are not guilty of the murders, though you are in some way connected with them. You have nothing to hide. And you are bound by honor to tell all you know. An innocent man is now in prison, charged with the crime."

"So help me God," he said after a pause, "I *will* tell you all I know. I *am* innocent, and I will make a clean breast of it."

What he told us was this. He had lately made a voyage to the East Indian islands. On the island of Borneo, he had, with the help of a friend, captured the orangutan. He had trouble with the beast on the home voyage, but at last got it safely inside his own place in Paris. Here he kept it hidden until it should get over a foot wound caused by a splinter on board the ship. He planned to sell the beast as soon as it was well.

In the early hours of the morning of the murder, he came home from a sailors' frolic, to find that the beast had broken out of the closet where it had been kept. It was in his bedroom, sitting before a looking glass and, razor in hand, was going through the motions of shaving. It had no doubt watched through the keyhole of the closet as its master shaved. The man was shocked to see the animal free, and holding a razor. He picked up a whip, which he used to quiet the creature when it fell into a mood of fury. At sight of the whip, the orangutan sprang through the door, down the stairs, and into the street, still holding the razor. The man followed, and the chase went on for some time. The streets were quiet, as it was near three o'clock in the morning. The ape was going down an alley in the rear of the Rue Morgue when its eyes were caught by a light shining from a fourth-story window. Rushing to the building, it climbed up the lightning rod, grasped the shutter thrown open against the wall, and swung itself through the window onto the bedstead, kicking the shutter open again as it entered.

The man followed up the lightning rod, urged on by his hope that now the ape was trapped, and by fear of what it might do in the house. He reached the window, but he could not swing the distance from the rod to the shutter, as the ape had done. The most he could do was to reach over so as to get a glimpse into the room. At this glimpse he nearly lost his hold, from horror of what he saw. Now it was that those awful screams arose upon the night. Madame L'Espanaye and her daughter, dressed in their night clothes, had been going through some papers in the iron safe, which had been wheeled into the middle of the room. They must have been sitting with their backs to the window and, judging from the time that passed between the entry of the beast and the sound of screams, did not at once see it. The flapping of the shutter they could have thought caused by the wind.

As the sailor looked in, the giant ape had seized Madame L'Espanaye by the hair and was moving the razor across her face, in the manner of a barber. The daughter lay on the floor in a faint. The screams and struggles of the old lady angered the brute, and with one mighty swing of its arm, it cut the head almost from the body. The animal then sprang upon the fainting girl and gripped her by the throat. Its wild glances at this moment chanced to fall on the face of its master outside the window, where rigid with horror, he still clung to the lightning rod. The beast remembered the dread whip, and its fury at once changed to fear. It skipped about the room in nervous activity, throwing down and breaking furniture, and dragging the bedding from the bed. (The voices heard by the party that had broken into the house, were the sailor's words of horror, and the jabbering was the voice of the ape.) At last it seized the corpse of the young woman and thrust it up the chimney, as if to hide its deed. It then picked up the body of the old lady and hurled it headlong through the window.

The sailor, fearing the outcome of this business, glided down the lightning rod and hurried home, giving up all thought of catching the beast. The ape must have left the room by the lightning rod just before the door was broken open by the police. Either it closed the window after it had passed through, or the window sash dropped of its own weight.

Dupin and I went to the police with the story of the murders, and Le Bon was at once set free. But the Prefect of Police was not entirely pleased that the case had been solved outside his office. He made some tart remarks about people minding their own business.

"Let him talk," said Dupin. "I have had the pleasure of beating him on his own grounds."

It only remains to be said that the beast was later caught by the owner himself, and he was able to sell it for a large sum to a zoo.

The Purloined[1] Letter

In Paris, just after dark one gusty evening in the fall, I was enjoying a smoke with my friend Auguste Dupin. We were sitting silent in his little back library, busy with thought, watching the curling smoke waves.

I was thinking of that affair of the Rue Morgue, which Dupin had solved for the police. In fact, I was thinking of the Prefect of Police when the door of our apartment opened and he walked in.

We gave him a hearty welcome, for he was one to be smiled at rather than scorned, and we had not seen him for some time. We had been sitting in the dark when he came in, and Dupin rose to light the lamp. But on hearing the Prefect say that he had come to get an opinion on some police business, Dupin sat down again.

"We can think over the problem better in the dark," he said.

"That is another of your odd notions," said the Prefect, who had a way of calling everything *odd* that was beyond his understanding. He thus lived in a world of *odd* affairs.

"Very true," said Dupin, as he handed the visitor a pipe and rolled toward him an easy chair.

[1] Stolen.

"And what is troubling you now?" I asked the Prefect. "Nothing in the way of murder, I hope."

"Oh, no. Nothing of that nature. The fact is the business is *very* simple. I am sure we of the police can handle it ourselves, but I thought Dupin would like to hear of the case, because it is so very *odd*."

"Simple and odd," said Dupin.

"Why, yes—well, not exactly that either. But the fact is, we have all been a good deal puzzled, because we have not yet been able to solve a problem so simple."

"Perhaps you are at fault because it *is* so simple," said Dupin.

"What nonsense you *do* talk!" said the Prefect, with a hearty laugh.

"Perhaps the mystery is a little *too* plain to be seen," said Dupin.

"Oh, good heavens! Who ever heard of such an idea?" Our visitor roared with laughter.

"But, after all," I said, "what *is* this case about?"

"Why, I will tell you," said the Prefect, as he gave a long, steady, thoughtful puff and settled himself in his chair. "But before I begin, let me warn you that the matter must be kept very secret. I should probably lose my office if it were known that I have spoken of it to anyone."

"Go on," I said.

"Or not—as you like," said Dupin.

"Well, then, I have had a personal report, from a *very* high quarter,[2] that a letter of the greatest importance has been stolen from the royal apartments. It is known who stole it. He was seen to take it. It is known also that he still has it."

"How is that known?" asked Dupin.

"Well, the letter gives its holder a certain power, and he has made use of this power."

"Still I do not understand," said Dupin.

[2] The queen, perhaps.

"No? Well, if the letter should come into the hands of a third person[3] —who shall be nameless—it would touch the honor of the royal person from whom it was stolen. This fact, you see, gives the holder of the letter a power over her."

"But who would dare—"

"The thief," said the Prefect, "is the Minister D——. He dares all things."

"And how did the Minister D—— get the letter from its proper owner?"

"His method was both cunning and bold. The letter had come to this royal person while she was alone in the royal apartments. While she was reading it, the other royal person came into the room. From this person, above all, she wished to keep the letter. She did not have time to put it out of sight in a drawer. She was forced to lay it, open as it was, upon a table, as if it were a matter that might be known to everyone. At this moment, in comes the Minister D——. His sharp eyes saw the letter at once, and he knew the handwriting. During some talk of state business, he laid some papers on the table by the letter. He went on talking about public affairs for some fifteen minutes. At last, he rose to go and picked up his papers from the table, taking with them the letter. The true owner saw, but dared not speak in the presence of the third person who stood by her. Thus the minister walked out with the letter. The power that he thus gained he has used for political pressure for some months. At last, the true owner of the letter was driven to come to the police, or rather to me."

"And a wiser agent," said Dupin, amid a cloud of smoke, "I suppose could not be found."

"You flatter me," the Prefect said. "But some such thought may have led her to put the matter in my hands."

[3] The king, perhaps. The Prefect does not dare to name names or to speak more plainly, because the matter touches royalty. The letter was perhaps a love letter to the queen.

"And what have you done to get back the letter?" I asked.

"My first care was to search the minister's house, and without his knowing of it. For, beyond all things, I have been warned not to let the minister know that the matter has been put into the hands of the police."

"But," I said, "are you not quite within your right in making the search? The Paris police have done this thing often enough before."

"Oh, yes. And it is easy to make the search unknown to the minister, for he is often away from home all night. He keeps no great number of servants, and they sleep at a distance from the master's rooms. Besides, I have keys, as you know, with which I can open any door in Paris. During the past three months I have searched the minister's house many times. The fact is, my honor depends on solving this problem. And—another great secret—the reward offered is very great indeed. So, I have searched the house until I am led to believe that the thief is more cunning than I, for I have not found the letter."

"Then clearly the letter is not in the house," I said. "Perhaps he carries it about in his pocket."

"He has been twice waylaid as if by robbers, and searched, at my orders," said the Prefect.

"You might have spared yourself that trouble," said Dupin. "The minister, I take it, is not *altogether* a fool, and would have thought of that danger."

"Not *altogether* a fool," said the Prefect, "but then he is a poet, which I take to be the next thing to a fool."

"True," said Dupin, after a long and thoughtful whiff at his pipe, "although I have written a few verses myself."

"Suppose you tell us the method of your search," I said to the Prefect.

"Why, the fact is, we took our time, and we searched *everywhere*. I know how to carry out such a search. We took the entire building, room by room. We opened every drawer. Of course you know that to a trained police officer, there can be no *secret* drawer. He will notice every amount of space—or bulk—in every cabinet. We took the chairs and probed the cushions with fine, long needles. We took off the table tops."

"Why so?" I said.

"You can lift off the top of a table, hide a small article in the cavity that the legs fit into, then put the top back. Bedposts may be used the same way, and of course any flat-topped piece of furniture."

"But you never could have taken to pieces *all* the furniture—at least without a lot of noise. And a letter may be made into a small roll no larger than a pencil. It might in that form be stuck into the rung of a chair. You did not take all the chairs to pieces?"

"No, we did better. We looked at the rungs of every chair, the joints of all the furniture, through a powerful magnifying glass. They had not been touched."

"I suppose you looked to the mirrors, between the glass and the boards. And you probed the beds and bedding, as well as the curtains and carpets."

"That of course. And we looked at the house itself. We divided the walls, ceilings, and floors into squares, and numbered these, so none might be overlooked. We went over every square inch. In the same way we went through the two houses standing beside the minister's."

"The two houses standing beside!" I cried. "You have indeed gone to great trouble."

"The reward offered is very great," said the Prefect.

"You looked at the grounds about the houses?" I asked.

"All the grounds are paved with brick. They gave us little trouble. We looked only at the moss between the bricks, and found it had not been moved."

"You looked among the minister's papers, of course, and into the books of his library?" I said.

"We opened every package. We turned over every leaf in

each book. And we measured the thickness of every book *cover* and looked at it through the magnifying glass."

"You looked into the cellars?"

"Yes."

"Then," I said, "you are searching in the wrong place, for the letter is *not* in the house, as you think."

"I fear you are right there," said the Prefect. "And now, Dupin, what would you advise me to do?"

"To search the house again."

"But as sure as I breathe, the letter is not at the house."

"I have no better advice to give," said Dupin. "You have, of course, a good description of the stolen letter?"

"Oh, yes!" Here the Prefect took from his pocket a notebook, and read aloud a description of the letter. Soon after, he left, more low in spirits than I had ever seen the good fellow before.

In about a month he visited us again. He took a pipe and a

chair, and we talked for some time of other things. At last, I said:

"And what of the stolen letter?"

"Well, I searched the house again, as Dupin advised—it was labor lost, as I knew it would be."

"How much was the reward offered, did you say?" asked Dupin.

"Why, a great deal—a *very* great reward. I don't like to say just how much. But one thing I *will* say, I would be willing to give my personal check for fifty thousand francs to anyone who could get me that letter. The matter is causing more trouble every day, and the reward has been doubled. But if it were trebled, I could do no more than I have already done."

"But I really think," said Dupin, speaking slowly, between whiffs at his pipe, "I really think—you might do—a little more, eh?"

"What do you mean?"

"Well, once upon a time, a certain rich miser tried to get from his doctor, without pay, some advice as to his illness. He described his ills as if they were those of a friend, then said, 'Now, doctor, what would you say my friend ought to take?' The doctor answered, 'Why, he should take *advice*, to be sure.'"

"But," said the Prefect, a little dashed. "I am *entirely* willing to take advice, and to pay for it. I would really give fifty thousand francs to anyone who would help me in this matter."

"In that case," said Dupin, opening a drawer and taking out a checkbook, "you may write a check for that sum. When you have signed it, I will hand you the letter."

I was dumb with surprise. The Prefect seemed thunderstruck. He sat still, silent, with open mouth and staring eyes. Then he took a pen, and after several pauses and vacant stares, wrote a check for fifty thousand francs, and handed it across the table to Dupin.

Dupin looked at the check carefully, put it in his pocket-book, then unlocked a drawer and took from it a letter, which he gave to the Prefect. That officer grasped it in a perfect agony of joy, opened it with trembling hands, glanced through it, and then rushed out of the room without saying another word.

When he had gone, Dupin told me all about it.

"The police of Paris," he said, "are able men in their way. They are cunning, and tireless in working along what they believe to be a proper method. Thus, when the Prefect told about his method of searching the minister's house, I knew he had done the work well, by *his method*."

"By his method?" I said.

"Yes. His method was not the best, but it was well carried out. Had the letter been where the police looked, the fellows would without doubt have found it."

I laughed—but he seemed quite serious in what he said.

"The fault," he said, "was that the method did not fit the case or the minister. The Prefect has a method that he uses in *all* cases, and with *all* men."

"What do you mean?" I asked.

"I will explain by telling you a story. Perhaps you know the simple game called 'even or odd.' One player, holding a number of marbles in a closed hand, asks another whether the number held is even or odd. If the guess is right, the guesser wins one marble. If wrong, he or she loses one. Once when I was a boy, I won all the marbles in school at this game. Of course I had a *method* of guessing, but I *changed* the method to suit the one I was playing with. For example, say I was playing with a very simple fellow. He holds up his closed hand and asks, 'Are they even or odd?' I answer by chance, 'Odd,' and lose. I then say to myself, 'The simpleton had the marbles even the first time; he will have them odd next time.' I therefore guess 'Odd,' and win. Now, when playing with a more clever boy, I would change the method. I would say to myself, 'Since I guessed odd the first time

53

and lost, the clever boy will at first thought expect me to guess even the second time, and he will therefore plan to hold an odd number. But on second thought, he will fear that this too simple change from the one to the other, will be just what I am expecting. He will therefore keep the marbles even, I guess 'Even,' and win. The schoolboys of course said that I was lucky. But was it merely luck?"

"No," I said, "you put yourself in the place of the other person, to learn what *his* method would be."

"That is where the police fail. They think only of their own method. In searching for anything hidden, they look only where they themselves would have hidden it. They are right this far—their own method of thought is that of the mass of people. But when they try to match their wit with one more cunning, they fail.

"Take, for example, this case," went on Dupin. "The Prefect took it for granted that all men go about hiding a letter—if not in a hole bored in a chair leg—in some other out-of-the-way hole or corner. And of course those are the first places searched. Anything so hidden can always be found, merely by looking carefully and long enough. But the Prefect was trying to outguess a man whose wit was greater than his. The minister would know that his house would be searched while he was away. He would not therefore hide the letter in any out-of-the-way hole or corner. He would find the most *simple* place to hide it. You will remember how the Prefect laughed the first time he visited us, when I said the matter might be too *plain* to be seen."

"Yes," I said, "I really thought he would kill himself laughing at the idea."

"I was sure that the minister had hidden the letter by the simple method of not trying to hide it at all. Full of the idea, I put on a pair of green glasses one fine morning, and called at the minister's house. He was at home, and we talked of various things, among them of my need to wear dark glasses. I was all the time looking keenly about me. I looked carefully at a large writing table near where he sat. It held a number of letters and other papers, and a few books. But the letter was not there. But from a little brass knob beneath the mantel piece, hung a card rack, held by a dirty blue ribbon. In this rack, which had three or four pockets, were five or six calling cards and one letter. The envelope was soiled and crumpled. It was torn nearly in two in the middle—as if someone had started to destroy it as worthless, had paused in the act, and then got rid of it by sticking it in the card rack."

"Did this letter agree with the Prefect's description of the stolen letter?" I asked.

"Not at all. The seal of this letter was large and black, with the D—— family's coat of arms. The seal of the stolen letter was small and red, with the S—— family's coat of arms. This letter was addressed to the minister, in the small neat writing of a woman's hand. The stolen letter was addressed to a certain royal person in a hand large and bold. But these very differences, and seeing the letter so soiled and torn, in full view of every visitor, the dirt on the ribbon and card-rack—so different from all else about the room—all this set me thinking. Perhaps all this was to lead one to view the thing as worthless."

Dupin paused for a thoughtful whiff at his pipe. I waited without speaking.

"I stayed with the minister as long as I could," went on Dupin, "keeping up a lively talk. During the time, I managed to get a good look at the letter. When I said good-bye to him and left, I purposely forgot my gold snuffbox lying on the table. The next morning I called to get the snuffbox, and stayed for more talk. Suddenly, as we were talking, we heard a pistol shot just under the window of the house, then screams and shouts. The minister rushed to the window, threw it open and looked out. I stepped quickly to the card rack, took the letter, put in its place another letter, which I had brought with me, made to look on the outside like the stolen letter. Then I followed him to the window. The

trouble was soon over. It had been caused by persons in my pay. Soon after, I left."

"But why did you replace the letter with another looking like it?" I asked.

"The minister is a man of nerve," said Dupin, "and has about him persons ready to do his every command. Had I been caught in the act, the good people of Paris might never have heard of me again."

STORIES OF HORROR AND FEAR

The Black Cat

The Cask of Amontillado

A Descent Into the Maelstrom

The Fall of the House of Usher

The Pit and the Pendulum

The Black Cat

I do not expect you to believe what I am about to write. Only a madman would expect it. Yet mad I am not, and very surely I do not dream. But tomorrow I die, and I would give the world my story, as plainly and frankly as if I were writing a story of everyday events. I will not try to explain my deeds. Later, perhaps, some person wiser, more calm than I, may see in this story that I tell, only the usual chain of events—cause leading to outcome.

From my childhood I was noted for gentleness and kindness. My playmates would laugh at me for being so tender-hearted. I loved animals, and my parents let me keep many pets. I spent most of my time with these pets, feeding and looking after them.

I married early, and was happy to find in my wife the same liking for pets. We had birds, goldfish, a fine dog, rabbits, a small monkey, and a cat.

The cat was beautiful, large, black, and so very knowing that my wife said he caused her to believe the old story that black cats are witches in disguise. Pluto—this was the cat's name—was my own pet and playmate. I alone fed him, and he followed me wherever I went about the house. It was hard to keep him from following me through the streets.

Our friendship lasted several years. But during this time my general nature was changing for the worse. The change in me was due to the use of (I blush to say it) strong drink. I grew more moody day by day, more selfish and careless of others. I spoke harshly to my wife, and at last I would even strike her. My pets, of course, suffered because of this change in me. I failed to feed and care for them, and ill-used

59

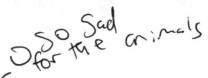

them in other ways. At first, I still felt kindly toward Pluto, though I never failed to vent my ill-temper on the rabbits, the monkey, and even the dog, whenever they were led by love or chance to come in my way.

My ill-nature grew upon me—for what can so change one from his better self as drunkenness? At last even Pluto, who was now getting old and somewhat peevish—even Pluto began to feel my ill-temper. One night, after coming home drunk, from one of my haunts about town, I thought that the cat tried to keep away from me. This made me angry. I grabbed him, and he, in fright, bit me on the hand. At once the fury of a demon filled me. My better self seemed to take flight from my body. A fiend-like, gin-fed evil thrilled my whole frame. I took from my pocket a pen-knife, opened it, grasped the poor beast by the throat, and cut one of its eyes from the socket! I blush, I burn, I shudder as I think of it.

When reason came back with morning—when I had slept off the night's drunkenness—I felt regret, half of horror, half of pity, for what I had done. But it was, at best, only a feeble regret. My soul was not touched. I again plunged into drink and soon drowned in wine all memory of the deed.

In the meantime the cat slowly got over the attack. The socket of the eye, it is true, was fearful to look on, but he no longer seemed to suffer any pain. He went about the house as usual, but, as might be expected, fled in terror at sight of me. I had enough of my old heart left to be pained, at first, to see this fear in a pet which had once so loved me. But this feeling soon gave place to anger. One morning, in cool blood, I slipped a noose about the cat's neck and hung it to the limb of a tree in the garden.

That night I was roused from sleep by the cry of fire. The curtains of my bed were in flames; the whole house was blazing. It was by a narrow chance that my wife, a servant, and I got out of the burning building. Everything was burned. All my worldly wealth was gone.

On the day after the fire I went to see the ruins. All the walls had fallen in, except one that had stood about the middle of the house and against which had sat the head of my bed. This wall had not burned as others because the plaster had been lately put on. A crowd of people were standing there looking at the wall with eager interest. I heard the words "strange!" "queer!" I went nearer and saw a figure, as if it had been drawn on the wall, of a gigantic cat with a rope about its neck.

When I first saw this strange figure, I was terrified. Then I remembered that the cat had been hung in the garden next to the house. Upon the cry of fire, this garden had filled with people. Some of them must have cut the animal from the tree where it was hanging and thrown it through an open window into my room. This had been done, perhaps, to rouse me from sleep. The falling of other walls had pressed the cat into the freshly spread plaster and thus the picture had been made.

Although I was thus able to explain the strange fact to myself, it cast a shadow upon my mind. For months I could not rid myself of the sight, and during this time, there came back a feeling that seemed like, but was not, sorrow for my crimes. I went so far as to look about the vile haunts where I now spent my time for another pet like the one I had killed.

One night, as I sat half drunk in a den of more than evil, I noticed some dark object lying upon the top of one of the great hogsheads of gin, or rum, which was the chief furniture of the place. I had been looking steadily at the top of this hogshead for some minutes, and I was surprised that I had not noted the object sooner. I went up to it and touched it with my hand. It was a black cat—a very large one—fully as large as Pluto, and very much like him in every way but one. Pluto had not a white hair upon any part of his body, but this cat had a large spot of white covering nearly the whole of the breast.

When I touched him, he got up at once, purred loudly,

rubbed against my hand, and seemed pleased with my notice. This, I thought, was the very cat I had been looking for. I at once offered to buy it of the landlord. But he made no claim to it—knew nothing of it—had never seen it before.

I went on stroking the cat, and when I left to go home, it showed a willingness to follow me. I allowed it to do so, now and then stooping and patting it as I walked along. When it reached the house, it made itself at home, and at once became a great favorite with my wife.

For my own part, I soon began to dislike it. I do not know how or why it was—but its very fondness for myself rather disgusted and annoyed me. By slow degrees these feelings grew into bitter hate. I kept away from the creature, not wishing to harm it, for memory of my former cruelty roused in me a certain shame. For some weeks I did not strike it. But gradually—very gradually, I came to look upon it with such loathing that I would turn away quickly from sight of it.

What I did not learn until the morning after I brought the cat home, was that it had, like Pluto, lost one of its eyes.

This fact, no doubt, added to my hatred of the beast. But it caused my wife to feel pity and to show the animal even greater kindness. Her nature, as I have already said, was marked by gentleness and kindness, qualities which had been a part of my nature once, and the source of many of my simple and purest pleasures.

The more I disliked this cat, however, the more it seemed to attach itself to me. The way it kept always close on my heels, I can never make the reader feel. Whenever I sat, it would crouch beneath my chair, or spring upon my knees and press on me its loving attention so hateful to bear. If I rose to walk, it would get between my feet and thus nearly throw me down, or fasten its long sharp claws in my clothes and climb up my body. At such times I longed to kill it with a blow, but was kept from doing so partly by memory of my former crime, but chiefly—let me confess it at once— by *dread* of the beast.

It is hard to tell what this dread was. I am almost ashamed to own—yes, in this prison cell, I am almost ashamed to own what it was that raised this dread within me. My wife had spoken more than once of the white spot on the animal's breast, which was the only mark of difference between this beast and Pluto. The outline of this spot began to change, by slow degrees—so slow that for a long time I would not believe that a change was taking place, except in my fancy. At last the spot took the outline of an object that I shudder to name—a hideous—a ghastly thing—the GALLOWS! It was, above all, because of this that I loathed and dreaded the creature. I would have rid myself of the monster *had I dared.*

And now was I indeed wretched. Alas! neither by day nor by night knew I the blessing of rest any more! During the day, the creature left me no moment alone. During the night I awoke from fearful dreams to find the hot breath of *the thing* upon my face, and its vast weight—a nightmare that I had no power to shake off—always upon my *heart!*

Under torments such as these, the feeble good within me

The Black Cat

[handwritten: I think the man has problems]

[handwritten in left margin: Omg so not cool!!]

died, Evil thoughts became my sole companions—the darkest and most evil of thoughts. I grew to hate all things and all mankind. I would give way blindly to sudden outbursts of fury, and my gentle wife, alas, was the most usual sufferer.

One day she went with me upon some household errand into the cellar of the old house, which our poverty drove us to live in. The cat followed me down the steep stairs and, getting under my feet, nearly threw me headlong. This roused me to madness. In my wrath I forgot the dread that had hitherto kept me from killing the beast. Raising an ax, I aimed a blow at the animal that would have been fatal had not my wife caught my arm to stop me. Her act threw me into the rage of a demon. I tore my arm from her grasp and buried the ax in her brain. She fell dead upon the spot, without a groan.

This awful murder being done, I set myself with thoughtful care to the task of hiding the body. I knew I could not take it from the house, either by day or by night, without the risk of being seen by the neighbors. Many plans came into my mind. I thought of cutting the corpse into small bits and burning them. Then of digging a grave for it in the floor of the cellar. Then of throwing it into the well in the yard. Or packing it in a box and getting a porter to take it from the house. At last I hit upon what seemed the best plan of all. I would wall it up in the cellar.

The walls of the cellar had been lately covered with a rough plaster, which the dampness of the place had kept from drying hard. In one of the walls was a fireplace, which had been filled up with brick and plastered over. I could easily take out the bricks at this place, put the corpse within, and wall up the place as before, so that no eye would notice any change.

And in thinking so, I was right. By means of a crowbar, I pulled out the bricks, propped the body against the inner wall, and with little trouble relaid the bricks as before. Then with great caution I got mortar, sand, and hair, and made

64

a plaster which could not be told from the old. With this, I very carefully went over the new brick work. When I had finished, I felt that all was right. The wall showed no sign of having been broken into. The rubbish on the floor was picked up with the greatest care. I looked around, and said to myself, "Here, at least, then, my labor has not been in vain!"

Next I looked about for the beast, which had been the cause of this wretched crime. I had made up my mind to put it to death. Had I been able to find it at the moment, I would have killed it. But it seemed that the crafty animal had been alarmed by my anger, and was keeping out of my way for a while. It is not possible to describe the deep sense of rest that I felt, now that the hated creature was out of my sight. It did not come during the night—and thus for one night at least I slept soundly. Yes, *slept*, even with the burden of murder upon my soul!

The second and the third day passed, and still my tormentor came not. Once again I breathed as a free man. The monster had fled forever! I should never again see the hated thing! I was happy! The guilt of my dark deed troubled me but little. Some few questions had been asked, but these had been easily answered. Even a search had been made—but of course nothing was to be found. I was safe.

The fourth day after the murder, a party of the police came and again made a search of the place. I felt quite safe, however, sure that my careful work had not been in vain. The officers had me go with them in their search. They overlooked no nook or corner. At length, for the third or fourth time, they went down into the cellar. I quivered not a muscle. My heart beat calmly. I folded my arms upon my chest and walked easily to and fro until the police were satisfied and ready to leave. Then joy in my heart was too strong. I longed to speak, if but one word, of my success, and to make doubly sure that they should believe me innocent.

"By the by, gentlemen," I said, as they turned to go up the steps, "this is a very well-built house." In the wish to say something easily, I scarcely knew what I spoke at all.

"These walls—are you going?—these walls are solidly put together." And here, in a sort of wild boasting, I rapped with my cane upon the very brick work that hid the corpse of my wife.

But may God keep me from the fangs of the Arch-Fiend! No sooner had the sound of my blows sunk into silence, than I was answered by a voice from within the tomb! It was a cry, at first muffled and broken, like the crying of a child, and then quickly rising into one long, loud scream—unlike anything human—a howl—a wail—a shriek.

Almost fainting, I staggered back across the cellar. For one moment the men at the stairs stood still, as in terror or awe. Then a dozen stout arms were tearing at the wall, and in a few moments the corpse was before our eyes. Upon its head, with red, wide-open mouth, and single eye of fire, sat the hideous beast that had caused me to do the murder, and whose voice had now given me to the hangman. I had walled the monster up within the tomb!

The Cask of Amontillado[1]

The man Fortunato had done me a thousand wrongs. I bore them as best I could. But when he began to insult me, I vowed revenge. You who understand my nature, will know that I spoke no threats aloud. But to myself I vowed to be avenged, *sometime.* The point was settled in my mind. And since I had vowed revenge *without fail,* I must take no risk. I must not only punish, but punish without hurt to myself. I would not be truly avenged if I brought harm upon myself as well as upon him. Nor would I be *completely* avenged unless *he knew* that his punishment came from me.

Neither by word nor deed did I give Fortunato cause to doubt my good will toward him. I smiled in his face, as always, and he did not know that *now* I was smiling at thought of the punishment sure to be his.

He had a weak point—this Fortunato—though in all other things he was a man to be looked up to, and even feared. He prided himself on being a good judge of wine. He was vain on this point. Fortunato was a quack in painting and gems, but in the matter of old wines, he was a good judge. I should know, for I too am a judge of Italian wines.

It was about dusk one evening during carnival time, that I met Fortunato. He greeted me with great warmth, for he had been drinking much. He was dressed in the spirit of carnival, wearing a tight-fitting jester's costume, gay with many-colored stripes. On his head was a high, pointed cap

[1] A kind of wine, named after Montilla, a town in southern Spain.

with bells. I was so pleased to see him that I thought I should never be done shaking his hand.

"My dear Fortunato," I said, "it is lucky we met. How well you are looking today. I have just bought a cask of what passes for amontillado, but I have my doubts that it is the real thing."

"Amontillado?" he said. "A cask? Impossible! And in the middle of the carnival!"

"I was silly enough to pay the full amontillado price. I should have asked your opinion, for I had my doubts. But you were not to be found, and I was afraid of losing the bargain."

"Amontillado!"

"I am not sure of it. I should like your opinion. But if you are too busy, I will get Luchesi's advice. If anyone is a good judge, he is. I am on my way to him now."

"Luchesi cannot tell amontillado from sherry."

"And yet some fools will say that his taste is as good as your own."

"Come, let us go."

"Where?"

"To your vaults."

"My friend, no—I would not trouble you. You are in a hurry. And Luchesi will—"

"I am in no hurry—come on."

"My friend, no. I see you have a severe cold, and the vaults are very damp."

"Let us go anyway. My cold is nothing. Amontillado! You have been fooled. And as for Luchesi, he can't tell sherry from amontillado."

As he spoke, Fortunato put on a mask of black silk and took my arm. I let him hurry me on to my place.

There were no servants at home; they had all gone off to make merry in the carnival season. I had told them that I should not return until morning and that they were not to leave the house. This was enough, I knew, to cause them to leave the place, one and all, the moment my back was turned.

I took two torches from their holders, and gave one to Fortunato. Then I bowed him through several rooms to the archway that led into the vaults. I passed first down the long winding stairway, warning him to be careful as he followed. We came at last to the foot of the stairway, and stood together upon the damp ground of the catacombs[2] of the Montresors.[3]

Fortunato's step was unsteady, and the bells on his cap jingled as he walked.

"The cask," he said. "Ugh! ugh! ugh!—ugh! ugh! ugh!"

"It is farther on," said I. "How long have you had that cough?"

He turned toward me, and looked into my face with the moist eyes of a drunken man. He could not reply for some minutes because of his cough.

"Ugh! ugh! ugh!—ugh! ugh! ugh! It is nothing," he said at last.

"Come," I said firmly, "we will go back. Your health is precious. You are rich, admired, loved. You are happy, as once I was. You are a man to be missed. For me, it is no matter. We will go back; you will be ill, and I would be blamed. Besides, there is Luchesi—"

"Never mind," he said; "the cough is a mere nothing; it will not kill me. I shall not die of a cough."

"True—true," I said, "and, indeed, I do not wish to alarm you—but you should take care of yourself. A drink of this Médoc[4] will defend you from the damp."

---

[2] An underground place for burial, made in the form of narrow rooms with alcoves set in the walls for tombs. Since wines are stored underground, there are found here both tombs and stores of wine.

[3] The name of the narrator's family. Both men belong to noble and rich families.

[4] A type of wine, named for the place it is made, Médoc, in southwest France.

Here I knocked off the neck of a bottle which I took from a row that lay upon the mold.

"Drink," I said, handing him the wine.

He raised it to his lips with a leer. He paused and nodded to me, making the bells jingle.

"I drink," he said, "to the peaceful rest of those that lie buried all about us."

"And I to your long life."

He again took my arm, and we walked on.

"These catacombs," he said, "go on a long way."

"The Montresors," I replied, "were a great family."

"I forget the motto of the Montresors' coat of arms."

"*Nemo me impune lacessit.*"[5]

"Good!" he said.

The wine sparkled in his eyes and the bells jingled. My own fancy grew warm with the Médoc. We had passed through long walls of piled skeletons, and long walls of casks and bottles, now one, now the other. At last we entered the deepest part of the vaults. I paused again, and this time I made bold to take hold of Fortunato's arm above the elbow.

"We are below the river's bed," I said. "Moisture drips among the bones. Come, we will go back before it is too late. Your cough—"

"It is nothing," he said. "Let us go on. But first, another drink of the Médoc."

I broke and handed him a bottle of De Grâve.[6] He drank it at a breath, laughed and threw the bottle upward, with a gesture I did not understand. I looked at him in surprise. He repeated the gesture—a strange one.

"You do not understand?" he said.

"No," I replied.

"Then you are not of the brotherhood—you are not of the masons."[7]

---

[5] "No one injures me with impunity."

[6] A wine made in the Gironde district of France.

[7] Fortunato is thinking of the brotherhood of Freemasons.

"Yes, yes," I said, "yes, yes."

"You? Impossible! A mason?"

"Yes, a mason," I replied.

"A sign," he said, "give the sign."

"It is this," I said, taking a trowel[8] from under my cloak.

"You jest," he cried, drawing back. "But let us go on to the amontillado."

"Be it so," I said, putting the tool under my cloak and again offering him my arm.

He leaned on it heavily. We passed through a range of low arches, went downward, passed on, went down again, and came to a deep vault in which the air was so foul our torches seemed to glow rather than flame. At the farther end of the vault was another, a smaller one. Three sides of this vault were lined with human bones, piled to the top. On the fourth side, the bones had been thrown down and lay in a heap upon the ground. In this wall cleared of bones, could be seen an alcove, six or seven feet high, about three feet wide, and four feet deep. It was formed between two pillars that held the roof of the catacombs, and was backed by one of their circling walls of solid stone. It seemed to have been made for no particular use.

"Go in," I said. "The amontillado is in here. As for Luchesi—"

Fortunato lifted his dull torch and tried to see what was in the alcove, but the light was too feeble.

"Luchesi knows nothing," he said, as he stepped unsteadily forward, while I followed at his heels.

In a moment he had reached the end of the alcove, and finding himself stopped by the rock wall, stood stupidly, at a loss. A moment more and I had chained him to the rock. Two iron rings were fixed in the wall; from one hung a short chain, from the other a padlock. It was the work of a few seconds to throw the chain about his waist and fasten it to

---

[8] A tool used by a bricklayer or mason, to spread mortar.

The Cask of Amontillado

the wall with the padlock. He was too much surprised to struggle. Taking the key from the lock, I stepped back out of the alcove.

"Pass your hand over the wall," I said. "You cannot help feeling the mold. The wall is *very* damp. Once more let me *beg* you to return. You will not? Then I must leave you. But I will first do what little I can for you."

"The amontillado!" he cried, still lost in wonder.

"True," I said, "the amontillado."

As I spoke these words I was busy among the pile of bones heaped on the floor. Throwing them aside, I soon came upon building stone and mortar. With these, and by use of my trowel, I began rapidly to wall up the opening to the alcove.

I had scarcely laid the first row of stones when I knew that Fortunato's drunkenness had largely worn off. The first sign of this was a low moaning cry. It was *not* the cry of a drunken man. There was then a long dogged silence.

I laid the second row of stones, and the third, and the fourth, and then I heard the chain rattling furiously. The noise lasted for several minutes. And so that I might the more enjoy the sound, I stopped my work and sat down upon the heap of bones. When the clanking at last stopped, I took up the trowel and laid the fifth, sixth, and seventh row of stones. The wall was now nearly upon a level with my breast. I again paused and, holding the torch over the wall, threw a feeble light upon the figure within.

The loud and shrill screams which burst suddenly from the throat of the chained form seemed by their force to thrust me violently back. For a moment I paused, trembling with fear. I drew my sword and began to grope with it about the alcove, but on second thought I was calm again. I placed my hand upon the solid wall of the catacombs and lost all doubt. I replied to his yells—I aided, I outdid him in the strength of loud cries. I did this, and the clamor grew still.

It was now midnight, and my task was drawing to a close.

I laid the eighth, the ninth, the tenth, and a part of the eleventh row of stones. There was lacking only a single stone. I struggled with its weight, and set it partly in place. But now there came from within a low laugh that raised the hair upon my head. It was followed by a sad voice, a voice unlike that of the noble Fortunato:

"Ha! ha! ha!—he! he! he!—a very good joke indeed—a fine joke. We will have many a good laugh about this—he! he! he!—over our wine—he! he! he!"

"The amontillado," I said.

"He! he! he!—he! he! he!—yes, the amontillado. But isn't it getting late? They will be waiting for us, the Lady Fortunato and the rest. Let us be going."

"Yes," I said, "let us be going."

"*For the love of God, Montresor!*"

"Yes," I said, "for the love of God!"

But to these words I listened in vain for a reply. I tired of waiting. I called aloud, "Fortunato!"

No answer. I called again, "Fortunato!"

No answer still. I pushed a torch through the opening and let it fall within. There came forth in return only a jingling of the bells. My heart grew sick—because of the dampness of the place. I hurried to finish my work. I forced the last stone into place; I plastered it up. Against the new masonry, I rebuilt the wall of bones. For the half of a century no mortal has moved them. *In pace requiescat!*[9]

---

[9] May he rest in peace.

A Descent into the Maelstrom[1]

We had now reached the very top of the highest crag. For some minutes the old man seemed too tired to speak.

"Not long ago," he said, "I could have guided you up this way as well as my youngest son could. But about three years ago, something happened to me that never before happened to mortal man. Or, at least, it never happened to man who lived to tell of it. The six hours of deadly terror which I then bore have broken me up, body and soul. You think me a very old man—but I am not. It took less than a single day to change these hairs from a jet black to white, to weaken my limbs, and to unstring my nerves so that I tremble at the least effort and am frightened at a shadow."

He threw himself down to rest on the edge of a cliff that rose straight for some fifteen or sixteen hundred feet from the sea below us. Nothing would have led me to go closer to the brink of the cliff than half a dozen yards. In truth, I was so fearful that I fell at full length upon the ground, clung to the grass about me, and dared not even glance up at the sky. I struggled hard to get rid of the idea that the base of the crag might be in danger from the fury of the wind. I could not, at first, reason myself into courage to sit up and look out into the distance.

"You must get over these fears," said the guide, "for I have brought you here to show you the scene of the event

[1] A famous whirlpool off the west coast of Norway.

that I spoke of. I shall tell you the whole story with the scene just under your eyes. We are now close upon the coast of Norway—in the dreary country of Lofoden. We are on top of Mount Helseggen, the Cloudy. Now raise yourself a little higher—hold on to the grass if you feel giddy—that's it. Now look out, beyond the belt of vapor beneath us, out into the sea."

I looked, and saw dizzily a wide spread of ocean, whose troubled waters seemed almost inky dark. To the right and left, as far as the eye could reach, there lay stretched out—like the wall of the world—a line of steep, black cliffs. The surf was howling and shrieking, as it forever reared its white crest high up against the black walls. About two miles out, lay a small island, craggy and barren. Still farther out, five or six miles, lay another island, marked by a wilderness of surge about it. So strong a gale was blowing landward that a small ship which lay to, in the distance, plunged her whole hull out of sight at every tug of the blast. Still, that part of the ocean which lay between us and the distant island, had nothing like a regular swell, but only a short, quick angry cross-dashing of water in every direction. Of foam there was little except near the rocks.

"The island in the distance," said the old man, "is called Vurrgh. The one midway is Moskoe. Do you hear anything? Do you see any change in the water?"

As the old man spoke, I noticed a sound, gradually growing louder, like the moaning of a vast herd of buffaloes upon an American prairie. At the same time I noticed that the chopping water beneath us was rapidly changing into a current which set eastward. Even as I gazed, the current took on a mighty speed, faster and faster, each moment adding to its headlong dash. In five minutes, the whole sea, as far out as Vurrgh, was lashed into a fury. But it was between Moskoe and the coast that the main uproar held its sway. Here the vast bed of waters, broken by a thousand currents, had burst suddenly into a heaving, boiling, hissing whirl.

In a few minutes more, there came over the surface another great change. The water grew somewhat smooth, but covered with great streaks of foam. These streaks spread out to great distance, mingled together, and took on a vast circling motion, forming a whirl more than a mile across. At the edge of the whirl was a broad belt of gleaming spray. Within was a terrific funnel, a wall of water—as far as I could see—smooth and shining and jet-black, sloping toward the horizon at an angle of forty-five degrees, speeding dizzily round and round, and sending forth to the winds its awful voice, half shriek, half roar. I threw myself on my face and clutched at the ground.

"This," said the old man, "is the great whirlpool of the Maelstrom. Between Lofoden and Moskoe, the water is thirty-six to forty fathoms[2] deep. When it is flood, a stream runs up the country, between Lofoden and Moskoe, with a mighty rush, but the roar of its mighty ebb to the sea sounds like a dreadful cataract, and the pits or whirls will suck in a ship and carry it down to the bottom and there beat it to pieces against the rocks. When the waters grow quieter, bits of the wreck float up to the surface. Periods of quiet come only at the turn of the ebb and flood, and in calm weather, and last only about fifteen minutes. Not only ships, but sometimes whales come too near the stream and are caught. No one could describe their howlings and bellowings as they struggle helplessly to get away. A bear once, trying to swim from Lofoden to Moskoe, was caught by the stream and carried down, while his terrible roars could be heard on shore. Large fir and pine trees, after being sucked into the whirl, rise again bristling with splinters. This shows that the bottom has craggy rocks, among which the trees have been whirled to and fro."

I could never give even the faintest idea of the size and the horror of the scene—or of the wild sense of *the strange,*

---

[2] A fathom is six feet.

which makes the onlooker dumb with awe. As to the depth of the water, I could not see how it could have been measured at all in the region of the whirlpool. Looking down from high above, I could not help smiling at the story of whales and bears being helpless in its force. It was plain that the largest ship, coming within reach of its sucking force, could no more keep away from it than a feather can hold against a hurricane.

"The whirlpool," said the old man, "is formed by the clashing of waters rising and falling against a ridge of rock and shelves which hems the water. Thus, the higher the flood rises, the deeper must the fall be, and the natural result is a whirlpool. There is, regularly, high and low water, every six hours. You have now had a good look at the whirl, and if you will creep round this crag, so as to get in its lee[3] and deaden the roar of the water, I will tell you a story about this whirlpool."

I did as he asked, and he began his story.

"I and my two brothers once owned a fishing boat of about seventy tons, which we used in fishing between the islands of Moskoe and Vurrgh. In all choppy water, there is good fishing, if one has the courage to go there for it. But among all the Lofoden coastmen, we were the only ones who would risk going out into that region. But for our risk, we often got in a single day more than other fishermen could scrape together in a week.

"We kept the boat in a cove about five miles higher up the coast than here. In fine weather, we would push across the main channel of the Maelstrom during the fifteen minutes of slack water, passing over far above the whirlpool. Then we would drop down upon some point where the eddies are not too strong. Here we would fish until time for slack water again, and then make for home. I could not tell you a small part of the dangers we met on the fishing ground—it is a bad spot to be in, even in good weather. But we made shift always to get through the Maelstrom itself without harm, although at times my heart was in my mouth, when we happened to be a minute or so behind or before the time for slack water. My oldest brother had a son eighteen years old, and I had two strong boys of my own. These would have been great help at such times. But, somehow, although we

---

[3] The side sheltered from the wind.

ran the risk ourselves, we had not the heart to let the young ones go into the danger—for it *was* a horrible danger, and that is the truth.

"On the tenth of July, 18—, a day which the people here will never forget—the wind blew the most dreadful hurricane that ever came out of the heavens. And yet all the morning, and indeed until late in the afternoon, there had been a gentle and steady breeze from the southwest, while the sun shone brightly. The oldest seaman among us could not have foreseen what was to follow.

"The three of us—my two brothers and myself—had crossed the channel of the Maelstrom about two o'clock in the afternoon. We soon had the boat nearly loaded with fine fish. When my watch showed seven, we started for home, expecting to cross the Maelstrom during slack water, which all knew would be at eight. For some time we spanked along at a great rate, never dreaming of danger. All at once, we were taken aback by a breeze from over Mount Helseggen. This was most unusual—something that had never happened to us before—and I began to feel a little uneasy, without exactly knowing why. We could make no headway at all. Looking back, we saw the whole horizon covered with a strange copper-colored cloud that rose with great speed. Then the breeze that had headed us off fell away, and we were dead becalmed, drifting about in every direction.

"In a few minutes the storm was upon us. Such a hurricane as then blew, the oldest seaman in Norway never saw anything like. At the first great puff, both our masts went by the board, as if they had been sawed off—the mainmast taking with it my youngest brother, who had lashed himself to it for safety. How my elder brother escaped I cannot say, for I never had a chance to learn. For my part, I threw myself flat on deck, with my feet against the timbers of the boat, and my hands grasping a ringbolt near the foot of the foremast. It was mere instinct that led me to do this—the best thing I could have done—for I was too flurried to think.

"Our boat was the lightest feather of a thing that ever sat upon water. It had a complete flush deck, with only one small hatch near the bow, and this hatch we always fastened down when about to cross the Maelstrom. Except for this, we should have gone down at once.

"I was trying to collect my senses, when I felt a grasp upon my arm. It was my brother's hand, and my heart leaped for joy, for I had thought he was overboard. He put his mouth close to my ear and screamed out the word 'Maelstrom!' I knew well enough what he meant by that one word—with the wind that now drove us on, we were bound for the whirlpool of the Maelstrom, and nothing could save us!

"When crossing the channel of the Maelstrom, we always went a long way up above the place of the whirlpool, even in calmest weather, and there waited and watched carefully for the slack. But now we were driving right upon the whirlpool itself, and in such a hurricane as this! To be sure, I thought, we shall get there just about the time of slack water. But I knew very well that we were doomed—that the mightiest ship afloat would have been doomed.

"By this time, the first fury of the tempest had spent itself, or perhaps we did not feel it so much, as we scudded before it. But at all events, the seas, which at first had been kept down by the wind, and lay flat and frothing, now rose like mountains. A change had come over the heavens, too. In all directions around, it was still black, black as pitch, but nearly overhead, there burst out, all at once, a round rift of clear sky—as clear as I ever saw—and of a deep bright blue. And through the rift, the moon shone with a brightness I never before knew her to wear. She lit up everything about us—but, oh, God, what a scene it was to light up!

"I now tried to speak to my brother—but the din had grown so great I could not make him hear a single word, although I screamed at the top of my voice in his ear. He shook his head, pale as death, and held up a finger, as if to say 'Listen!' At first, I could not make out what he meant—

then a hideous thought flashed upon me. I looked at my watch by the moonlight—it was not going! *It had run down at seven o'clock. We were behind the time of slack, and the whirl of the Maelstrom was in full fury!*

"When a boat is well built, properly trimmed and not deep laden, the waves in a strong gale seem to slip from beneath her—and this is what is called *riding,* in sea phrase. So far, we had ridden the swells. But now a mighty sea bore us up—up—up—as if into the sky. I would not have believed that any wave could rise so high. And then down we came with a sweep, a slide, and a plunge that made me feel sick and dizzy, as if I were falling from some lofty mountain top in a dream. But while we were up, I had thrown a quick glance around—and that one glance was enough. I saw the whirlpool, about a quarter of a mile dead ahead—but after the hurricane, oh, so unlike the everyday whirl, I closed my eyes in horror. The lids clenched themselves together as if in a spasm.

"Two minutes afterward, I felt the waves suddenly grow quieter. I opened my eyes and saw that we were in the midst of foam. Then the boat made a sharp half turn, and shot off in a new direction, swift as an arrow. The roaring noise of waters was drowned in a kind of shrill shriek. We were now in the belt of surf that always surrounds the whirl. I thought another moment would plunge us into the funnel, down which I could see only dimly, because of the great speed with which we were wheeled along. The boat seemed to skim like an air bubble upon the surface.

"It may seem strange, but now that we were in the very jaws of the whirlpool, I felt more composed than when we were nearing it. Having made up my mind to hope no more, I got rid of a great deal of my terror. I began to think how grand it was to die in such a manner, how foolish to think of so small a matter as my own life, when in the grip of such a power. I even felt a *wish* to see the depth of the whirl itself, even at the cost of my life. And my chief regret was that

I should never be able to tell my old friends on shore about the wonders I should see. Strange fancies to come to mind at such a time! Since then, I have thought I must have been a little dizzy, from the whirling of the boat.

"Another thing that caused me to be more composed was that now the wind was not tearing at us. If you have never been at sea in a heavy gale, you can have no idea of how the wind and spray together can blind, deafen, and strangle you, and thus hinder your power to think or act.

"How many times we circled in the belt of foam, I cannot say. We went round and round perhaps an hour, flying rather than floating, getting slowly more and more into the middle of the belt, and nearer to its horrible inner edge. All the time I had never let go of the ringbolt. My brother was at the stern, holding on to a small empty water cask which had been lashed to the deck, and was the only thing on deck not swept off when the gale first struck.

"As we neared the brink of the pit, my brother let go his hold upon the cask, and made for the ring, which I held. In the agony of his terror, he tried to force my hands away, as it was not large enough for both to hold. I never felt deeper grief than when I saw him do this, although I knew he was a madman, made so by sheer terror. I did not hold out against him; in a few minutes it would not matter whether either of us held on at all. I let him have the ringbolt, and went to the cask. It was not hard to make this move, for the boat flew round steadily enough. But I was scarcely in the new place, when the boat gave a wild lurch headlong into the funnel.

"As I felt the sickening downward sweep, I tightened my hold upon the barrel and closed my eyes. For some seconds I did not open them—while I wondered that I was not already in my death-struggle with the water. But moment after moment passed. I still lived. The sense of falling was over, and the motion of the vessel seemed about the same as when we were in the belt of foam. I took courage and opened my eyes.

A Descent into the Maelstrom

"The boat seemed to be hanging, as if by magic, midway down within a vast funnel. Its smooth ebony-like sides, sloping at an angle of more than forty-five degrees, spun around with dizzy speed. The rays of the moon, shining through that rift in the clouds, streamed in a flood of glory along the black walls, and down into the depth far below. The boat rode upon the whirling walls as upon an even keel, and I held my place on deck almost as easily as if we had been upon a dead level. This, I suppose, was owing to the speed at which we whirled.

"Although the rays of the moon seemed to reach to the very bottom of the funnel, I could make out nothing clearly there, because of a thick mist, over which hung a bright rainbow. The mist or spray was no doubt caused by the clashing of waters at the bottom of the funnel. The whistling shriek that went up out of that mist I dare not try to describe.

"Round and round we swept—not with a steady motion—but in dizzy swings and jerks that sent us sometimes only a few hundred yards, sometimes nearly the complete circle. Our movement *downward* at each whirl was slow, but noticeable.

"Our boat was not the only object in the grip of the whirl. Both above and below us, I saw trunks of trees, broken boxes, barrels, pieces of wreckage, ships' masts. I began to watch the many things that floated in our company. I saw that all things did not sink toward the pit of the funnel at the same rate. Then I called to mind the many different objects that lay along the coast of Lofoden, which had been swallowed up by the whirlpool and later thrown forth again. Most of these were shattered, but I remembered that *some* of them had not been broken up at all. Now I was able to understand this difference. Those objects that had not been broken in the whirlpool had entered the whirl at so late a period of the tide, or for some reason had gone down so slowly, that they did not reach the bottom before the turn of the flood or ebb came. In either case, such objects might be whirled

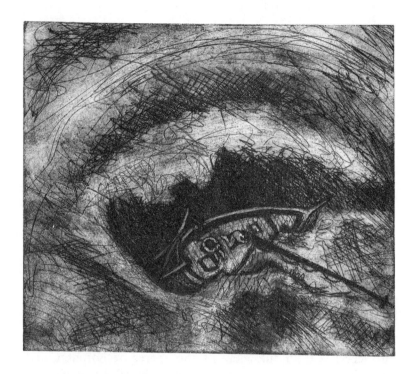

up again to the surface without going the full length of the funnel into the pit.

"Watching the floating objects circling about, I noticed three things. First, as a rule, the larger the object, the more rapidly it went down. Second, objects that tended to be round or ball-like went down faster than objects of other shapes. Third, objects shaped like a cylinder went down slowly. Several objects of this general shape—barrels, masts of ships—which had once been on our level were now high above us. Now I knew what I should do. I would lash myself to the watercask I now held, cut it loose from the deck, and throw myself with it, into the water.

"I got my brother's attention by signs, pointed to floating barrels that came near us, and did all I could to make him understand what I was about to do, and why. I thought that at last he did understand. But whether he did or not, he shook his head and would not let go of the ringbolt. With a bitter pang, I left him to his fate, fastened myself to the cask by the ropes that had been used to lash it to the deck, and threw myself with it into the sea.

"After I had left the boat, I kept watching it, for my brother was still on it. As we circled, it sank down, down, until it was far below me. It might have been an hour after I had left the boat, when I saw it suddenly make three or four wild whirls, and plunge headlong into the foam of the very bottom, bearing my brother with it. The barrel to which I was fastened had now sunk about half the distance between the spot where I had left the boat, and the bottom of the funnel.

"About this time, I began to see a change in the funnel. The slopes of the sides became less steep, the speed of the whirl grew less, the mist and the rainbow began to leave, and the bottom of the funnel seemed to rise.

"The sky was clear, the winds had gone down, and the moon was setting in the west, when I found myself on the surface. I was in full view of the shores of Lofoden, and just above the spot where the whirlpool of the Maelstrom *had been*. It was the hour of the slack, but the sea still heaved in waves mountain high. In a few moments the current hurried me down the coast into the fishing grounds of the fishermen of Lofoden.

"I was picked up by my old mates—but they did not know me. My hair, which had been raven black the day before, was as white as you see it now. They say, too, that my whole outward look had changed. I told them my story—they did not believe it. I now tell it to *you*—and I can scarcely expect you to put more faith in it than did the merry fishermen of Lofoden."

The Fall of the House of Usher

I had been traveling alone, on horseback, during the whole of a dull, dark, and soundless day in the autumn of the year. After passing through a dreary tract of country, I came at last, as evening drew on, in sight of the house of Usher. As I looked upon the house—the bleak walls, the vacant eye-like windows, upon a few rank sedges and the white trunks of decayed trees—I felt a sinking of the heart. I checked my horse at the brink of a lake that lay dark and still by the walls of the dwelling. Looking down, I saw the same scene thrown back by the still, black water—the gray sedge, the ghostly tree stems, and the eye-like windows.

But to this mansion of gloom I had come to stay for some weeks. Its master, Roderick Usher, had been one of my good friends in boyhood, though years had passed since our last meeting. A letter from him had come to me—in a distant part of the country, a letter of distress, in which he spoke of being ill and of a great need to see me, his best and indeed his only personal friend. The way he begged me to come—the *heart* that went into his request, left me no choice. I set out at once.

As boys, we had been much together, yet I really knew little of him. It was not in his nature to give way to close friendship. I knew, however, that his family had been famous through long ages, in works of charity and of art. I knew, too, that the Usher race, time-honored as it was, had always lain in a direct line. Name and property had passed down from father to son. The family mansion had come to be known as the House of Usher, as if house and family were one and the same.

Now, as I paused and looked at the house, there grew in my mind a strange fancy. There seemed to be hanging over the entire place a leaden vapor, dull and faintly seen. Shaking off what *must* have been fancy, I looked more closely at the building. It was darkened by great age. But, although the stones were each crumbling with age, no part of the building had fallen. It stood wholly unbroken at every point. In this it made me think of old woodwork which has rotted for long years in a vault, but still stands whole so long as no breath of air moves it. However, a closer look at the building showed a crack that started at the roof and ran down the wall in a zigzag way until it became lost in the dull waters of the lake.

Pam Gomer

I rode over a short bridge to the house. A servant took my horse, and I entered a wide hall. Another servant, of quiet step, led me in silence through many dark and winding passages, toward the study of his master. On one of the stairways, I met the doctor of the family. His face, I thought, looked both puzzled and cunning. He spoke to me in a hurried, doubtful manner, and passed on. The servant now threw open a door and bowed me into the presence of his master.

The room I entered was large and lofty. The windows were long and narrow, pointed at the top, and set so high above the dark oak floor as to be altogether out of reach. Feeble gleams of light, coming through the narrow panes of colored glass, failed to light up the far corners of the great room. Dark curtains hung upon the walls. The furniture was plentiful but old, worn and without comfort. Books and music were scattered about, but failed to give any warmth to the place. An air of sorrow, of stern deep gloom, hung over all.

As I entered, Usher rose from a sofa where he had been lying, and greeted me eagerly. I thought at first that his welcome had in it something of the forced warmth of a bored man of the world. But a glance at his face told me that he was sincere.

I looked on him with a feeling half pity, half awe. Surely, a man had never before changed so greatly, in the same length of time, as had Roderick Usher. It was hard to believe that this was the same person who had been my boyhood friend. Yet his looks, even then, had been unusual—face pale, eyes large and very bright, lips somewhat thin but beautifully curved, nose large, chin finely formed but rather weak, hair of weblike softness, a forehead unusually wide.

His manner, I noticed at once, was one moment lively, the next uncertain. His voice changed from tones of trembling doubt to the hollow-sounding tones of sureness that may be heard from a drunk man.

He spoke of his great wish and need to see me, of the comfort he would have from my visit. He talked for some time of

89

his illness. "It is a family evil," he said, "one for which I can hope to find no cure." Then he added quickly, "A mere case of nerves, which no doubt will soon pass off. I suffer from senses too keen. I can eat only the most tasteless food. The odor of flowers seems to press upon me. My eyes cannot stand the light. I cannot bear the touch of certain kinds of cloth. As for sounds, the only ones that do not fill me with agony are those made by stringed and musical instruments." He paused a moment, and then went on. "Most of all, I am a bound slave to a terror of FEAR. I shall die in this folly. Thus, and no other way, will I be lost. I have no fear of danger, but only of terror. In my unnerved state, I feel that the time will come, sooner or later, when I must give up life and reason together, in some struggle with grim FEAR. I shudder at the very thought of any event that may act upon this terror of my soul, FEAR."

Sad!

I learned, moreover, another feature of his mental condition. He believed certain superstitions about the mansion in which he lived and had not left the place for several years. He felt that the very walls had a peculiar effect, indeed a *hold*, on his spirit and mind.

His illness was caused chiefly, he said, by his fear of losing his beloved sister, his only companion for years. Doctors did not know the nature of her illness; she seemed gradually to waste away.

"Her death," he said, with a bitter grief which I can never forget, "would leave me the last of the Ushers."

While he spoke, his sister, Lady Madeline, passed through a distant part of the room, without having noticed me. Her appearance filled me with awe and dread. Yet I could not say why or account for these feelings. When the door closed behind her, I turned to her brother, but he had covered his face with his hands. I saw that he had grown even paler than before, and tears trickled between his thin fingers.

That very evening she took to her bed finally—as her brother told me at night, with great feeling. The glimpse

I had of her was likely to be the last I should see of her living.
For several days after, she was not named by either Usher
or myself. During that time I was busy trying to cheer him.
We painted and read together, or I listened as if in a dream
to the wild music he created on his guitar. His long, sad songs
will ring forever in my ears. The words of one of these I have
remembered, for it was this song which told me that Usher
knew his reason was tottering. The verses ran very nearly
like this:

> In the greenest of our valleys,
>   By good angels tenanted,
> Once a fair and stately palace—
>   Radiant palace—reared its head.
> In the monarch Thought's dominion,
>   It stood there!
> Never seraph spread a pinion
>   Over fabric half so fair.
>
> Banners yellow, glorious, golden,
>   On its roof did float and flow,
> (This—all this—was in the olden
>   Time long ago);
> And every gentle air that dallied
>   In that sweet day,
> Along the ramparts plumed and pallid,
>   A winged odor went away.
>
> Wanderers in that happy valley
>   Through two luminous windows saw
> Spirits moving musically
>   To a lute's well-tuned law,
> Round about a throne where, sitting
>   (Porphyrogene!)[1]
> In state his glory well befitting,
>   The ruler of the realm was seen.

Weird

[1] Born to be a king.

91

The Fall of the House of Usher

And all with pearl and ruby glowing
　Was the fair palace door,
Through which came flowing, flowing, flowing,
　And sparkling evermore,
A troop of Echoes, whose sweet duty
　Was but to sing
In voices of surpassing beauty,
　The wit and wisdom of their king.

But evil things, in robes of sorrow,
　Assailed the monarch's high estate.
(Ah, let us mourn, for never morrow
　Shall dawn upon him, desolate!)
And round about his home, the glory
　That blushed and bloomed
Is but a dim-remembered story
　Of the old time entombed.

And travelers now within that valley,
　Through the red-litten windows see
Vast forms, that move fantastically
　To a discordant melody,
While, like a rapid ghastly river,
　Through the pale door
A hideous throng rush out forever
　And laugh—but smile no more.

I well remember that a discussion of this song led to a completely different topic. Usher held an opinion that awed me, not because it was strange, but because he seemed to believe it so strongly. He believed that plants could feel and know. He went so far as to believe that nonliving matter had the same power.

"I see signs of this," he said, "in the gray stones of this home of my fathers. Sometimes the place will gather about itself an air or vapor of its own."

I started when I heard him say this, for I had had the same strange fancy on the day I had first looked upon the old mansion

I watched him painting, and saw grow on the canvas, touch by touch, a vague something at which I shuddered, without knowing why. By the very nakedness of his drawings, he overawed. If ever mortal painted an idea, that mortal was Roderick Usher. One small picture showed the inside of a very long vault or tunnel, with low walls, smooth and white. Certain points of the picture gave the idea that this vault or tunnel was far beneath the surface of the earth. There was no outlet, no torch or other source of light; yet a flood of light rolled throughout, and bathed the whole in a ghastly splendor.

One evening, he told me suddenly that Lady Madeline had died. "I will not place the body in the family burial place at once," he said, "because her doctors have been very curious about her strange illness. I will place it for a time in one of the many vaults in the main walls of the building."

I called to mind the unpleasant face of the doctor I had met the day I came, and said nothing against the plan. I had no desire to oppose what I thought was a harmless, and by no means unnatural, precaution.

We two alone bore the body to the tomb. The vault in which we placed it was small, damp, without means of light. It lay at great depth, and was beneath that part of the building where was my own apartment. It had been used, it seemed, in former days as a prison, and later as a storage place for powder, for part of its floor and all the long archway leading to it, were lined with copper.

The heavy iron door, also copper lined, made a sharp, grating sound as it moved on its hinges. The place had been so long closed, the air was stifling. Having set down our mournful burden, we lifted the lid of the coffin and looked upon the face of Lady Madeline. She was so much like her brother I was startled. Usher, seeing this, murmured that they were twins, and bound to each other by an understanding that few could know.

We did not look long upon her, for we could not view the face of the dead without awe. The illness which had carried her off in youth had left the mockery of a faint blush upon the face and bosom, and that lingering smile so terrible upon the lips of the dead. We closed and screwed down the lid. After closing and locking the iron door, we went back to the hardly less gloomy rooms in the upper house.

And now, after some days of bitter grief, a change came over my friend. He moved about from room to room with hurried and unequal steps. He became, if possible, even paler than before, and the brightness was gone out of his eyes. A quaver, like the trembling of terror, marked his speech. Sometimes I felt that his mind was struggling for courage to give out some secret that bore him down. Again, at other times, I believed his strange manner was but the wanderings of a madman, for I saw him sit sometimes for long hours, his gaze vacant, as if closely listening to some sound that only he could hear. It was no wonder that his condition terrified me. I felt creeping upon me, by slow yet certain degrees, the wild influence of his fantastic superstition.

It was the night of the seventh or eighth day after placing Lady Madeline in the tomb. Sleep came not near me, while hour after hour went by. The dark curtains swayed fitfully to the breath of a rising storm, and rustled against the walls. Gradually my whole frame fell into a tremor, and my heart was weighed down by alarm. Shaking this off with a gasp and a struggle, I lifted myself upon the pillows and peered into the deep darkness of the room, listening to certain low and unknown sounds which came through the pauses of the storm.

I rose and threw on my clothes, for I felt I could sleep no more that night. I tried to overcome my fear by pacing to and fro in the room. Soon I heard a light step on the stair. A moment later Usher rapped at my door and came in, carrying a lamp. He seemed to be, as usual, pale and drawn—but, moreover, there was an air of restrained *hysteria* in his manner. But anything was better than being alone and I welcomed his presence as a relief.

"And you have not seen it?" he said, after staring about him. "You have not seen it? But wait, you shall."

He hurried to a window and threw it wide open to the storm. The fury of the gust nearly lifted us from our feet.

The Fall of the House of Usher

Dense clouds seemed to press down over the building, as the winds went whirling from all points against each other. There was no glimpse of the moon or stars, nor any flash of lightning. But the underside of the clouds, and all objects on the earth below, were glowing with the strange light of a vapor that hung about the mansion.

"You must not look at this!" I said, shuddering as I closed the sash and dragged Usher from the window to a seat. "These are but harmful vapors rising from the swamp about the lake. The air is chilling and dangerous to your health. Here is a book—I will read and you shall listen, and so we will pass away this terrible night together."

In truth, there was little in the book that could have interested the lofty mind of my friend. But it was the only book at hand, and I hoped his wild mood might be soothed by listening to any reading. It was an old story, and as I read I came to the following:

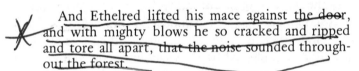

And Ethelred lifted his mace against the door, and with mighty blows he so cracked and ripped and tore all apart, that the noise sounded throughout the forest.

At the end of this sentence, I started, and for a moment paused. For it seemed to me that from some far away place in the mansion, there came faintly what might have been an echo of the very cracking and ripping sound I had read of. It was beyond doubt, I thought, only my fancy that heard such echo in the rattling windows and the many other noises of the storm. I went on reading:

And Ethelred entered and saw a dragon which sat on guard. He lifted his mace and struck upon the head of the dragon, which fell before him, with a shriek so horrid, harsh, and piercing that Ethelred was fain to close his ears with his hands against the dreadful noise of it.

Here again I paused, and now with a feeling of wildest wonder. This time there could be no doubt whatever that I heard a low, distant, harsh and grating sound, though where it came from I could not say.

Struck as I was by wonder and terror, I was careful not to excite my friend. I was not sure that he had noticed the sounds, although during the last few minutes his manner had strangely altered. He had gradually brought his chair around, so as to sit facing the door of the room. Thus I could see only part of his face. But I saw his lips tremble as if he murmured to himself. His head had dropped upon his breast—yet I knew he was not asleep, for his eyes stared wide open. He rocked from side to side with a gentle, even sway. I went on reading:

And now as Ethelred went over the silver pavement of the castle, the shield upon the wall fell down at his feet with a terrible ringing sound.

As these words passed my lips, I heard a distant clanging—as if a shield of metal had indeed at the moment fallen heavily upon a floor of silver. I leaped to my feet, but the regular rocking movement of Usher went on. I rushed to his chair. His eyes were fixed before him, his face was set like stone. As I placed my hand on his shoulder, a strong shudder ran over his body, and he spoke in a low hurried murmur. Bending closely over him, I drank in the awful meaning of his words.

"Yes, I hear it, and *have* heard it long—long—long. Many hours, many days have I heard it—yet I *dared* not—oh pity me, wretch that I am—I *dared* not speak! I told you my senses were keen—I *now* tell you that I heard her first feeble movements in the hollow coffin. I heard them—many, many days ago—yet I dared not—I *dared* not speak! *We have put her living in the tomb!* And now—tonight—the breaking of the door and the death-cry of the dragon, and the clang of the shield—say rather, the breaking of her coffin and the grating of the iron hinges, and her struggles in the coppered archway of the vault! Oh, where shall I fly! Will she not be here soon! Is she not now hurrying to blame me for my haste? Have I not heard her footstep on the stair?" Here he sprang to his feet and shrieked out his words as if in the effort he were giving up his soul, *"Madman! I tell you that she now stands outside that door!"*

The huge door to which he pointed drew slowly back at that moment. It was the work of the wind—but there, outside the door, there *did* stand the lofty figure of the Lady Madeline. Blood was upon her white robes, and signs of bitter struggle upon every part of her thin form. For a moment she stood reeling to and fro in the doorway. Then with a low moaning cry, she fell heavily inward in her final death struggle. She fell upon the body of her brother, and bore him to the floor, a corpse.

From that room and that mansion, I fled. The storm was still abroad in all its wrath. As I was crossing the old bridge a light suddenly shone along the way, and I turned to see where the gleam had come from. It came from the full and blood-red moon, and it shone through a broad crack which ran from the roof of the building, in a zigzag way, to the base. As I looked, the crack widened—then came a fierce breath of whirlwind, and my brain reeled as I saw the mighty walls rushing apart. There was a sound like the voice of a thousand waters—and the deep and dark lake at my feet closed sullenly and silently over the House of Usher.

The Pit and the Pendulum

(During the Middle Ages, the church and the state set up Courts of Inquiry to inquire into the religious opinions of anyone who might not be loyal to the established church. These courts were very severe in punishing those who did not accept the teachings of the church. Some courts used torture to compel confession, and non-believers were sometimes burned at the stake. So merciless were the Spanish courts that the term "Spanish Inquisition" had become a common term, meaning a too close inquiry or too harsh punishment.)

I was sick—sick unto death with that long agony. And when they at last unbound me and I was allowed to sit, I felt that my senses were leaving me. Those awful words—that dread sentence of death—were the last words of meaning that had reached my ears. After that the voices in the Court of Inquiry had become a dreamy meaningless hum, and soon I heard no more. Yet, for a while, I saw the lips of the black-robed judges—but in what horrible exaggeration! They seemed to me white—whiter than the paper on which I write these words—and thin, thin with a grim firmness, because in these judges was no pity for another's torture. I saw that words of my fate were still coming from those lips. I saw them writhe to form the awful words. I saw them shape themselves to speak my name, and I shuddered, for I heard no sound. I saw, too, for a few moments of wild horror, the

99

soft waving of the black curtains that covered the walls. And then my vision fell upon the seven tall candles upon the table. At first they seemed white slender angels, who would save me. Then, all at once, there came a most deadly sickness over me, and the candles seemed like ghosts with heads of flame, from whom would come no help.

And then there stole into my fancy, like a rich musical note, the thought of what sweet rest there must be in the grave. But at this moment the figures of the judges vanished, as if by magic, from before me. The tall candles sank into nothingness. Their flames went out utterly and silence, stillness, and night came upon me. I had swooned, but yet awareness was not entirely gone from me. Shadows of memory tell dimly of tall figures that lifted and bore me in silence down—down—still down—till a hideous dizziness pressed upon me at the mere idea of endless depth.

Very suddenly there came back to me a sense of motion and sound—the heavy beat of my heart sounding in my ears. Then the sense of being alive, without thought of any condition of living. Then very suddenly *thought*, and shuddering terror, and struggle to recall my true state. Then a strong wish to slip again into darkness and nothingness. Then a rushing return of life and a successful effort to move. And now a full memory of the trial, of the judges, of the black curtains, of the dread sentence, of the sickness, of the swoon and entire forgetfulness.

So far, I had not opened my eyes. I felt that I lay upon my back, unbound. I reached out my hand, and it fell heavily upon something damp and hard. I let it lie there for many minutes, while I tried to imagine where I could be. I dreaded the first glance at objects around me. It was not that I feared to look upon things horrible, but that I dreaded lest there should be *nothing* to see. At last, with a wild fear at heart, I quickly opened my eyes. My worst fear was realized—the blackness of eternal night was about me. I struggled for breath. The dense darkness seemed to bear down and stifle

the seems as if hes the fascinating

were closed

I did not know his eyes were closed

I'm not sure where me is right now

this man thinks a lot

me. The air was close. I lay quiet, trying to reason myself
into calm. I brought to mind the courtroom scene, and tried
to account for my being where I lay. The dread sentence had
been passed, and, as it seemed to me, a very long time had
passed since then. Yet not for a moment did I think myself
actually dead. But where and in what state was I? Had I been
taken back to my dungeon to await the date of execution?
But no, my dungeon, like all cells of the condemned at
Toledo, had windows of a kind to let in some bit of light.

A fearful idea now suddenly drove the blood in torrents
back upon my heart, and for a short time I sank again into
a swoon. When my senses returned, I at once started to my
feet, trembling in every fiber, I threw my arms wildly about.
I felt nothing, yet dreaded to move a step, lest I be stopped
by the walls of a *tomb*. Sweat burst from every pore, and
stood in cold big beads upon my forehead. I slowly moved
forward, with arms outstretched, eyes straining from their
sockets in the hope of catching some faint ray of light.
I went forward several paces, but still all was blackness and
vacancy. I breathed more freely. It seemed plain that mine
was not, at least, the most hideous of fates.

And now as I went slowly stepping forward, there came
to mind a thousand vague rumors of the horrors of Toledo
dungeons. I had heard strange things whispered of these
dungeons—fables I always thought them—but yet too fearful
to repeat save in a whisper. Was I left to die of starvation in
this deep underground world of darkness—or what fate,
perhaps even more dreadful, awaited me? That my fate
would be death, and a death of more than ordinary
bitterness, I knew my judges too well to doubt. The manner
and the hour of death were all that I was in doubt about.

My outstretched hand at last touched a wall, seemingly
of stone masonry, very smooth, slimy and cold. I followed
along the wall, stepping slowly with great care, but I could
not by this method learn the size of my dungeon, for I might
go around and around, not knowing when I again reached

101

I dont think its a good idea to bring a knife

the starting place. I therefore felt for the knife which had been in my pocket when I was taken into the court room, intending to force the blade into a crevice of the wall to mark my starting point. But the knife was gone; my clothes had been exchanged for a wrapper of coarse serge. I now thought of another plan. I tore a part of the hem from the robe and placed this strip of cloth at full length on the floor, and at right angles to the wall. In groping my way around the prison, I could not fail to step on this strip of cloth when the circuit was complete. But I did not know the size of the dungeon, or my own weakness. The ground was moist and slippery, and when I had staggered onward for some time I slipped and fell. In my great weariness, I lay there not trying to rise, and sleep soon overtook me as I lay.

Upon awaking, and stretching out an arm, I found beside me a loaf and a pitcher of water. I was too weak to think about the reason for this, but ate and drank eagerly. Soon afterward, I rose and went onward as before, and with much toil, I came at last upon the strip of cloth. Up to the point where I fell, I had counted fifty-two steps. After beginning my walk the second time, I had counted forty-eight more—when I reached the strip of cloth. There were in all, then, a hundred steps. Allowing two steps to the yard, I judged the dungeon to be fifty yards around. But I had met, however, many angles in the wall, and thus I could form no guess as to the shape of the vault, for vault I could not help supposing it to be.

I had little purpose—certainly no hope—in this effort to learn something of my prison, but a vague curiosity caused me to keep up the effort. Leaving the wall, I started to cross the room. At first I went with great caution, for the floor was slippery with damp and slime. At length, however, I took courage, and began to step forward firmly, trying to move in a direct line. I had gone some ten or twelve steps in this manner when the torn hem of my robe caught my heel, causing me to stumble till I fell violently, face forward.

102

So far this has all been him talking and thinking

In a moment, as I still lay flat on the floor, I was amazed at a strange condition. It was this: my chin rested upon the floor of the prison, but the upper part of my face touched—nothing. At the same time my forehead seemed bathed in a clammy vapor. I put forward my arm, and shuddered to find that I had fallen at the very brink of a circular pit, whose size I had no means of knowing, at the moment. Groping about the masonry just below the edge, I succeeded in breaking loose a small fragment, which I let fall into the pit. For many seconds I heard its echo as it dashed against the sides of the chasm in its fall. At length there was a sullen plunge into water, followed by loud echoes. At the same moment, there came a sound like the quick opening and closing of a door overhead, and a faint gleam of light flashed through the gloom, and as suddenly faded away.

I saw clearly the doom that had been prepared for me, a doom I had escaped by the timely accident of a fall. Another step before my fall, and the world would have seen me no more. I had been given a choice of death, either sudden death by dropping into the pit, or a slower, more horrible death.

By long suffering my nerves had been so unstrung that I trembled at the sound of my own voice. Shaking in every limb, I groped my way back to the wall. I would perish there rather than risk the terrors of the wells, for my imagination now pictured many of them, all about the dungeon. In another state of mind, I might have had courage to end my misery at once by a plunge into one of these pits, but now I was a weakling coward. And I could not forget what I had heard of the court's punishments—that *sudden* death was no part of their most horrible plans.

The excitement of fear kept me awake for many long hours, but at length I again slumbered. Upon arousing, I found by my side, as before, a loaf and a pitcher of water. I felt a burning thirst and drank the water without pausing. It must have been drugged—for scarcely had I drunk, before I became very drowsy. A deep sleep fell upon me—a sleep like that of death. How long it lasted, of course, I know not. But when once again I opened my eyes, the objects around me were visible. By some strange luster, the cause of which I could not at first learn, I was able to see about the prison.

As to its size I had been greatly mistaken. The distance around was not more than twenty-five yards. The reason for my error now flashed upon me. I had counted fifty-two steps up to the time when I fell. I must at that point have been within a step or two of the strip of cloth. In fact, I had gone almost around the vault when I fell asleep. Then, upon awaking, I must have turned and gone forward in the other direction—thus was I led to believe the vault to be nearly double the size it actually was. My troubled and weakened state had prevented me from noticing that I began with the wall to the left, and ended with the wall to the right.

104

I had been misled, too, as to the shape of the prison. In feeling my way in the dark, I had found many angles, and from this fact had formed the idea of a great irregularly-shaped room—so confusing is the effect of total darkness upon one suddenly roused from sleep or a swoon. I saw now that the general shape of the prison was square; the angles were simply those of a few niches that occurred here and there. And what I had mistaken for stone walls, seemed now to be iron, or some other metal, in huge plates, whose joints had caused the feel of masonry. On the walls were rudely daubed pictures of fiends with skeleton forms, in every attitude of threat. While the outlines of these monstrous figures were plain enough, the colors seemed faded and blurred, as if from the effects of a damp air. In the center yawned a circular pit, the one I had managed to escape, and the only one in the dungeon.

All this I saw dimly and by much effort—for my position had greatly changed during my slumber. I now lay upon my back, and at full length, on a kind of low wooden framework. To this I was securely bound by a long strap, which passed around and about my limbs and body, leaving free only my head and my left arm to such degree that I could reach for food from a dish which was on the floor by my side. I saw, to my horror, that the pitcher had been removed. I say to my horror, for I burned with a fierce thirst. It appeared to be the purpose of my tormentors to increase this thirst—for the food in the dish was highly seasoned.

Looking upward, I viewed the ceiling of my prison. It was some thirty of forty feet high. In one of its panels was painted the figure of Time, as he is commonly pictured, save that in place of a scythe he held what, at a casual glance, I supposed to be the pictured image of a huge pendulum such as we see on old clocks. There was something, however, in the appearance of the thing that caused me to look at it more intently. While I gazed up at it (for it was directly over me) I fancied that it moved. The next minute I knew that it

105

handwritten margin note (right): I think to myself sometimes

handwritten margin note (right): interesting .

handwritten margin note (bottom): ★ So far its not the best story (yes) ★

moved. It was swung by a weighty rod of brass, which, being short, made the sweep, of course, quite slow. I watched it for some minutes somewhat in fear, but more in wonder. Wearied at length with watching its dull movement, I turned my eyes away.

A slight noise drew my attention and, looking to the floor, I saw several very large rats running about. They had come from the pit which lay just within view to my right. Even as I gazed, more came trooping up, with hungry eyes, called by the scent of the food. From this, it took much effort and attention to scare them away.

It might have been half an hour, perhaps even an hour (for I could make no reliable guess as to the passing of time), when I again looked upward. What I saw stunned and amazed me. The sweep of the pendulum had increased by nearly a yard. As a natural result, its speed was also much greater, and it hissed as it swung through the air. As it had noticeably descended I now saw—with what horror it is needless to say—that its lower part was formed of a crescent of glittering steel, about a foot long from horn to horn, the horns upward, and the under edge seemingly as keen as that of a razor.

I could no longer doubt the doom prepared for me. The agents of the Court had learned that I had discovered the pit—*the pit*, whose horrors had been deemed fit to punish so bold an objector as myself—*the pit*, typical of hell, and regarded, so report whispered, as the most terrible of all their punishments. The plunge into this pit I had escaped by the merest chance. I knew that surprise, or entrapment into torment, was a planned part of all final punishment inflicted by the Court. Now that I had failed to fall, it was no part of the demon plan to hurl me into the pit—a different and a milder death awaited me. Milder! I half smiled in my agony as I thought of using such a word to describe the death in store for me.

Why tell of the long, long hours of horror during which I

counted the rushing sweep of the pendulum? Inch by inch—line by line—with a lowering that could be measured after what seemed an age—down and still down it came! Days passed—it might have been that many days passed—before it swept so closely over me as to fan me with its sweep. I could smell the odor of the sharp steel as it cut through the air just above me. I prayed heaven for a more speedy descent of the keen blade. I grew frantic and struggled to force myself upward against the sweep of its fearful edge. And then I became suddenly calm, and lay smiling at the glittering thing, as a child at some rare bauble.

There was another period of swoon. It was brief, for when I again returned to life, there had been no noticeable descent of the pendulum. But it might have been long—for I knew there were demons who took note of my swoon, and who could have stopped the pendulum during the time I lay unaware of its torturing descent.

I felt sick and weak as if from long starvation. Even amid the agonies of that time of torture, the human nature craved food. With painful effort I stretched out my left arm as far as my bonds allowed and took what food had been spared me by the rats. As I put a portion of it within my lips, there rushed to my mind a half-formed thought of joy—of hope. Yet what business had I with hope? Long suffering had nearly destroyed all my ordinary powers of mind. I was an imbecile—an idiot.

The sweep of the pendulum was at right angles to my length. The crescent was set to cross the region of the heart. Now it was fraying the upper surface of the serge of my robe—returning again and again to repeat the touch. Notwithstanding its wide sweep (some thirty feet or more), and the hissing vigor of its descent, still the fraying of my robe would be all that it would do for several minutes. At this thought I paused, for I dared not think of further stages of the descending sweep. It was as if, in keeping my mind on this stage of the descent, I could prevent the steel from

107

The Pit and the Pendulum

coming lower. To the right—to the left—far and wide—with the shriek of a damned spirit! to my heart, with the stealthy pace of the tiger! I laughed and howled; now one, now the other.

Down—certainly, ceaselessly down! It swept within three inches of my bosom. I struggled violently—furiously—to free my left arm, which was free only from the elbow to the hand. I could reach the platter beside me and put the food to my mouth, with great effort, but no farther. Could I have broken the fastenings above the elbow, I would have seized and tried to stop the pendulum. I might as well have tried to stop an avalanche!

Down—still down it came! I grasped and struggled at each sweep. My eyes followed its outward or upward whirls with the eagerness of unmeaning despair. They closed tightly as the whirl lowered, although death would have been a relief, oh, how unspeakable! Still I quivered in every nerve to think how slight a sinking of the machinery would send that keen, glistening ax through my bosom.

I saw that some ten or twelve sweeps would bring the steel into actual cutting contact with my robe, and suddenly there came over my spirit all the collected calmness of despair. For the first time during many hours—or perhaps days—I *thought*. It now came to me that the band that bound me was all in one piece. The first stroke of the razor-like crescent across any part of it would enable me to unwind it with my left hand. But how fearfully close at that stage would be the cutting steel. The slightest movement of my body upward, how deadly! Was it not likely, moreover, that my tormentors had foreseen this possibility? Did the bandage cross my bosom in the track of the pendulum? Dreading to have my faint hope destroyed, I so far lifted my head as to have a view of my breast. The band passed over and over my body and limbs, in all directions—save in the path of the destroying crescent.

Scarcely had I dropped my head back, when there flashed

upon my mind a thought or hope—feeble, dim, scarcely sane—but still completely formed. For many hours the low framework upon which I lay had been swarming with rats. They were wild, bold, hungry—their red eyes glaring upon me as if they waited but for all my movements to cease before making me their prey. "What food," I thought, "have they been trained to eat in the well?"

In spite of all my efforts to drive them away, they had eaten almost all the food on the dish. I had kept up a constant see-saw or wave of the hand about the platter, but at length, they gave less and less heed, as they became used to the regular motion. In their keen eagerness for food, they often sank their sharp fangs in my fingers. With the bits of oily and spicy food which still lay on the platter, I thoroughly rubbed the binding band about my body, wherever I could reach it. Then raising my hand from its place of guard over the food, I lay breathlessly still.

At first the hungry rats were startled at the change, and shrank back; many ran down into the well. But soon, seeing that I remained without motion, one or two of the boldest leaped upon the framework on which I lay, and smelled at the food-stained bands. This seemed the signal for a general rush. Forth from the well they hurried in fresh troops. They clung to the wooden frame—they overran it, and leaped in hundreds upon my body. The measured movement of the pendulum disturbed them not at all. Keeping out of its reach, they busied themselves with the food-smeared bands. They pressed—they swarmed upon me in ever larger and larger heaps. They writhed upon my throat. Their cold lips touched my own. I was half stifled by their thronging pressure. There is no word for the disgust that chilled my heart with a heavy clamminess. One minute more, and the struggle, I felt, would be over, for plainly I felt the loosening of the band. I knew that in more than one place it must be already gnawed in two. With more than human will power, I lay *still*.

At length I felt that I was *free*. The band hung in pieces

109

from my body. But the stroke of the pendulum already pressed upon my bosom. It had cut through the serge of the robe. It had cut through the linen beneath. Twice again it swung, and a sharp sense of pain shot through every nerve. But the moment of escape had come. At a wave of my hand, the rats hurried noisily away. Then with a steady movement—cautious, sidelong, shrinking, and slow—I slid from the bonds and beyond reach of the pendulum knife. For the moment, at least, *I was free.*

Free!—and in the hands of the Inquisition! I had scarcely stepped from my wooden bed of horror upon the stone floor of the prison, when the motion of the hellish pendulum ceased, and I saw it drawn up by some unseen force, through the ceiling. Plainly, my every motion was watched. Free!—I had only escaped one form of agony to learn of another form.

I rolled my eyes nervously around the walls that hemmed me in. For many minutes of dreamy and trembling groping, I tried to understand the nature of a change that had taken place in the prison room. Slowly I knew, for the first time, whence came the dim glow which lighted the cell. It came from a crack, about half an inch wide, which ran entirely around the cell at the base of the walls, which were thus completely separated from the floor. I tried, but of course in vain, to look through the opening.

As I arose from the attempt, the reason for the altered look of the place broke at once upon me. As I have already said, although the outlines of the pictured figures on the walls were plain, yet the colors were dim and blurred. These colors had now taken on a brightness that gave the fiendish pictures a look of reality that might have shaken firmer nerves than mine. Demon eyes glowed upon me from a thousand directions, where none had been seen before. They all now gleamed with a lurid luster of fire that I could not force myself to regard as unreal.

Unreal! Even as I looked, there came the odor of heated iron. A deeper glow settled each moment in the eyes that glared at my agony! A richer tint of crimson spread over the pictured horrors. I panted! I gasped for breath! There could be no doubt of the purpose of my tormenters, most demon-like of men! I shrank from the glowing metal toward the center of the cell.

Amid thoughts of the fiery death before me, the idea of the coolness of the well came over me like balm. I rushed to its deadly brink. The glare from the glowing roof lighted it to its inmost recesses. Yet, for a wild moment my mind refused to grasp what I saw. At length it forced—it wrestled its way into my shuddering reason. Oh! for a voice to speak! —oh! horror!—oh! any horror but this! With a shriek, I rushed from the edge of the well, and buried my face in my hands—weeping bitterly.

The heat rapidly increased, and once again I looked up,

shuddering as though from an intense fever. There had been a second change in the cell—and now the change was in the *form.* My tormentors, hurried by my two-fold escape, would have no more dallying with the King of Terrors. The room had been square. I saw that two of its corners had become acute angles, and the other two, of course, obtuse. The fearful difference quickly increased, with a low rumbling or moaning sound. The cell had now become diamond shaped. The change went steadily on, and I neither hoped nor wished it to stop. "Death," I said, "any death but that of the pit." Fool! I might have known that *into the pit* it was the purpose of the moving walls of burning iron to urge me! Could I resist either their glow or their pressure? And now flatter and flatter grew the diamond with a speed that left me no time for thought. Its center, which was of course its greatest width, came just over the yawning gulf. I shrank back—but the closing walls pressed me still onward. At length for my seared and writhing body there was no longer an inch of foothold on the floor of the prison. I struggled no more, but the agony of my soul found vent in one loud, long scream of despair. I tottered on the brink—I closed my eyes—

There was a clamor of human voices! There was a loud blast as of many trumpets! There was a harsh grating as of a thousand thunders! The fiery walls rushed back! An outstretched arm caught my own as I fell, fainting, into the gulf. It was that of General Lasalle. The French army had entered Toledo. The Inquisition was in the hands of its enemies.

✱ Wow this story was pretty good! ✱

PSYCHOLOGICAL STORIES

The Angel of the Odd
William Wilson

The Angel of the Odd

It was a chilly November afternoon. I had just eaten a very hearty dinner, and was sitting alone in the dining room, with my feet on the hearth. At my elbow was a small table, which I had pulled up to the fire, and on the table were bottles of wine and some food.

During the morning I had been reading some rather tedious books, and I now felt a little stupid. I tried to rouse myself by drinking wine, but that failing, I turned to a stray newspaper. I read the list of "houses to rent" and "dogs lost." I turned to the editor's page and read it from beginning to end, but could understand it no more than if it had been written in Chinese. I was about to throw the paper away when I noticed the following:

> A London paper reports the death of a person from a very strange cause. He was playing at "puff the dart," a game played by blowing a needle at a target by puffing the breath through a tin tube. He placed the needle at the wrong end of the tube, and drawing his breath strongly so as to puff the dart forward with force, he drew the needle into his throat. It entered his lungs, and in a few days killed him.

Upon reading this, I fell into a great rage, without knowing why. "The story is false, made up by one of those fellows who think up odd accidents to trick and gull the people. But to a thoughtful person, like me—" by force of habit I put my forefinger to the side of my nose—"it is plain that the oddest accident of all, is the *great number* of odd accidents that are printed in newspapers every day. For my part, I will believe nothing from now on that has anything odd about it."

"Mein Gott, den, vat a vool you be for dat!" said one of the strangest voices I ever heard.

At first, I thought it was a roaring in my ears, such as a person now and then has when getting very drunk. But on second thought, the voice was more like the sound made by beating an empty barrel with a big stick. I am not a nervous person, and the very few glasses of wine which I had sipped made me so bold that I felt no fear. I lifted my eyes and looked carefully around the room for the speaker. I could not see anyone at all.

"Humph!" said the voice, as I looked about me, "you must be so drunk as de pig, den, for not zee me at I zit at your zide."

Hearing this, I thought of looking right before my nose, and there, sure enough, right across the table from me, sat a very strange being. His body was a wine or rum cask. To its lower part, were fastened two kegs, which seemed to serve for legs. For arms, there dangled from the upper part of the cask, two rather long bottles, with the necks outward, for hands. All the head that I could see on the monster, was one of those canteens which look like a snuffbox with a hole in the middle of the lid. On top of the canteen was a funnel, like a cap slipped over the eyes.

The canteen was set on edge, with the hole toward me. Through this hole, which seemed puckered up like the mouth of a very strict old maid, was coming that rumbling sound which was the creature's voice.

"I zay," said he, "dat you must be pigger vool as de goose, not to pelief vat you zee in de print."

"Who are you?" I said, somewhat puzzled. "How did you get in here? And what are you talking about?"

"As vor how I comed here," said the creature, "dat is none of your pizziness. As for vat I talk about, I talk vat I tink proper. And as vor who I be, vy, dat is de very ting I comed here vor to let you zee vor yourzelf."

"You are a drunken beggar," said I. "I shall ring the bell and have my servant kick you into the street."

"He! he! he!" said the fellow, "dat you can't do."

"Can't do!" said I. "What do you mean? I can't do what?"

"Ring de pell," he said, trying to twist his vile little mouth into a grin.

Upon this, I started to get up, to go ring the bell. But the monster reached across the table very calmly and, hitting me on the forehead with the neck of one of his bottle-arms, threw me back into my chair. For a moment, I sat still, half stunned. He went on talking.

"You zee," he said, "it is best vor to zit still. And now you shall know who I be. Look at me! Zee! I am de *Angel of de Odd*."

"You are *odd* enough," I said, "but I always thought that an angel had wings."

"De ving!" he cried, very angry. "Vat I do mit de ving? Mein Gott! Do you take me vor a shicken?"

"No—oh, no!" I said, rather frightened, "you are no chicken—certainly not."

"Vell, den, zit still. Pehave yourzelf, or I'll rap you again mid my vist. It is de shicken hab de ving, und de owl hab de ving. De angel hab *not* de ving, and I am de *Angel of de Odd*."

"And your business with me now is—is—"

"My pizziness!" cried the thing, "vy, vat a low-bred puppy you must be vor to ask a gentleman und an angel about his pizziness."

This was rather more than I could bear, even from an angel. Getting up my courage, I picked up a salt shaker from the table and hurled it at his head. Either he dodged or my aim was poor, for all I did was to break the glass on the face of the mantel clock. As for the angel, he gave me two or three hard raps upon the forehead as before. These quieted me at once, and I am almost ashamed to say that either through pain or anger, a few tears came to my eyes.

"Mein Gott!" said the Angel of the Odd, seeming to soften at sight of my tears, "de man is eder ferry drunk or ferry zorry. You must not trink it so strong—you must put de vater in de vine. Here, trink dis, like a good veller, and don't cry now—don't!"

He filled up my glass, which was already a third full of wine, with a colorless fluid that he poured from one of his bottleneck hands. His kindness pleased me greatly, and I grew willing to listen to his talk. I cannot, of course, tell all that he said to me. But I learned from what he said that he looked after the awkward acts of mankind, those persons whose business it was to bring about the *odd accidents* that are always surprising people.

Once or twice, when I dared to say I doubted his office,

he grew very angry indeed, so at last I thought it wise to say nothing at all, and let him have his own way. He talked on and on, therefore, while I leaned back in my chair with my eyes shut, eating grapes and flipping the stems about the room. By and by the angel suddenly chose to see in my action a lack of respect for himself. He rose in a terrible rage, let his funnel-cap slip down over his eyes, swore a vast oath, spoke a threat of some kind, made me a low bow, and left, wishing me "many happy days and a little more good sense."

I was glad to see him go. The very few glasses of wine that I had sipped had made me sleepy, and I wished to take a nap of some fifteen or twenty minutes, as I always did after dinner. At six o'clock, I had a meeting, which I must not miss. The insurance on my house was up, and some question having risen about it, the officers of the insurance company had asked me to meet them at six, when we would settle the terms of the new contract.

Glancing up at the clock on the mantel—I was too sleepy to take out my watch—I was glad to see that I still had twenty-five minutes to spare. It was half past five. I could easily walk to the insurance company's office in five minutes. My usual after-dinner nap never lasted more than twenty-five minutes. I felt safe, therefore, to let myself drop off to sleep.

When I awoke and looked at the clock, I saw that I had not slept my usual fifteen or twenty minutes, but only three minutes. The clock still lacked twenty-seven minutes of six. I jumped up to look closer at the clock, and saw that it had stopped. My watch pointed to half past seven. I had slept two hours, and was too late for the meeting.

"Oh, well," I thought, "I can call at the office in the morning and explain. But what can be the matter with the clock?"

I soon saw that one of the grape stems which I had been flipping about the room, while talking with the Angel of the Odd, had flown through the broken glass over the clock face, and had lodged, oddly enough, in the keyhole of the face.

119

"Ah!" said I, "I see how it is. This thing speaks for itself. A natural accident, such as will happen now and then!"

I thought no more of it, and at my usual hour went off to my bedroom. Here, having set a candle upon a table at the bed head, I started to read a book, but fell asleep in less than twenty seconds, leaving the candle burning.

My dreams were full of visions of the Angel of the Odd. I thought he stood at the foot of the bed, drew the curtains aside, and in the hateful, hollow tones of a rum cask, threatened me with the bitterest punishment for having scorned him. He finished his long lecture by taking off his funnel-cap, sticking the smaller end of it into my throat, and thus flooding me with an ocean of water, which he poured from one of the long-necked bottles that served him for arms. I strangled in such agony that I woke.

There was a strong smell and smother of smoke, for a blaze was sweeping through the room, and had come so close as to burn off all my hair. Every door was blocked by the fire. A crowd, which had gathered quickly outside, brought a long ladder and raised it to my window. I was going down the ladder to safety, when a huge hog—whose large round stomach, in fact its whole form, caused it to look very much like the Angel of the Odd—suddenly took it into his head that his left shoulder needed scratching, and used the ladder for a rubbing post. Down came the ladder, with me on it. I fell so hard I broke my left arm.

The accident of the fire, and the danger to me—for, as I said, it had come close enough to singe off all my hair—and the accident of no insurance—all caused me to think very seriously. I made up my mind that I needed a wife. I offered my hand to a rich widow, who was at that time mourning the loss of her seventh husband. I knelt at her feet, and she bowed her rich tresses over mine, or rather over the wig that I was then wearing. I know not how the tangle took place, but so it was. I rose with a shining pate, wigless. Thus ended my hopes of the widow, by a very *odd accident.*

I looked elsewhere for a wife, and soon became engaged

to another lady. Meeting her one day in a crowded street, I was hastening to greet her with my best bow when a cinder caught in my eye and made me, for the moment, completely blind. Before I could get over the pain and open my eyes, the lady had passed on, lost to me, because of what she thought was an insult, my failure to greet her.

While I was standing still in pain and unable to see, the Angel of the Odd came up and offered his help. He looked at my eye and told me that I had a drop in it. Whatever a "drop" was, he took it out, and I was soon well.

But I had lost the lady and was ready to die. I went my way to the nearest river, took off my clothes, and threw myself headlong into the current. The sole witness of my act was a crow that had been eating fermented grain and had become drunk. The bird took it into its silly head to fly away with my trousers. Seeing the bird flutter off with that most necessary part of my costume, I forgot that I should soon have no need for clothes of any kind. I felt only that great urge to get back what was so necessary to correct dress and took off at full speed after the bird, with my nose in the air.

Not looking where I ran, I fell over a high cliff, and would have been dashed to pieces at the bottom, except for a very *odd accident.* A balloon was passing, and I was able to catch hold of a long rope that hung down from it. Hanging there, I cried out with all the power of my lungs to the man above in the balloon car. But for a long time either the fool could not, or the villain would not, see me.

Meantime the balloon went up and up, while my strength grew weaker and weaker. I was about to give up and drop gently into the sea, when I heard a hollow voice above me. It seemed to be lazily humming a tune. Looking up, I saw the Angel of the Odd. He was leaning, with his arms folded, over the rim of the car. He held a pipe in his mouth, and as he slowly puffed at it, seemed well pleased with himself and with the world. I was too weak now to speak, but begged him with my eyes to help me.

For several minutes, although he looked me full in the

face, he said nothing. At last he moved his pipe from the right to the left corner of his mouth and said:

"Who be you, und vat be you doing dare?"

My only answer was a weak cry of "Help!"

"Help?" he said; "not I. Dare is de pottle—help yourself."

And he let fall a heavy bottle which hit me on the crown of the head so hard I thought my brains were knocked out. I was about to let go of the rope and give up the ghost with a good grace, when he said:

"Hold on! Don't be in de hurry—don't! Do you vant de udder bottle, or have you got zober yet and come to your zenses?"

I made haste to nod my head twice—once to mean no that I did not want the other bottle, and once to mean yes that I was sober and had come to my senses. This seemed to soften the angel.

"Und you pelief in *me*, de Angel of de Odd?"

I nodded once more.

"Put your right hand into your left-hand breeches pocket, in token of your full pelief in de Angel of de Odd."

This I could not do. In the first place, my left arm had been broken in my fall from the ladder, and therefore if I put my right hand in my pocket, I would let go of the rope altogether. In the second place, the crow had carried off my breeches. So I had to shake my head, meaning I could not do as he ordered.

"Go to der teuffel, ten!" roared the Angel of the Odd. And so saying, he drew a sharp knife across the rope to which I clung, and cut it in two.

This happened just at the balloon was passing over my house (which had meantime been rebuilt), and it chanced that as I fell, I hit upon the chimney, tumbled headlong down it, and lit upon the dining room hearth.

Upon coming to my senses—for the fall stunned me—I saw that it was about four o'clock in the morning. My head lay in the ashes of a burned-out fire, and my feet rested on an overturned table. On the floor lay bits of food, broken glasses, and shattered bottles. Thus did the Angel of the Odd avenge himself.

William Wilson

My earliest memory of school life takes me back to a misty-looking village of England, where there were a great many large old trees, and where all the houses were very old. In truth, it was a dream-like and spirit-soothing place, that old town.

The grounds of the school were large. A high and solid brick wall, topped with a bed of broken glass, ran all around. Beyond this wall we went only three times a week. Once every Sunday afternoon we were taken for a short walk through some of the nearby fields. Twice during Sunday we were marched to service in the village church. The head of our school was pastor of this church. With what deep wonder did I see him, from my distant place in the gallery, march slowly into the pulpit. This holy man—could this be he of the sour face who, stick in hand, enforced the laws of the school?

Within the high wall was the playground. It was level, and covered with fine hard gravel. I well remember that it had no trees, no benches. Of course it was in the rear of the house. Before the house, the grounds were planted with shrubs. But through this region we passed very few times—such as the time we first entered the school, and the day we finally left it. Or, when a parent or a friend called for us, and we joyfully left for Christmas or summer holidays.

But the house—how quaint an old building was this—what a palace of magic! There was really no end to its windings. From one room to any other, there were sure to be three or four steps, leading up or down. It was hard to say, sometimes, which of its two floors one was on at the moment. Then, there were many wings—so turning and re-turning upon themselves, that my ideas about the mansion were about as vague as when I tried to understand the meaning of "the everlasting." During the five years I was there, I never knew for certain in what far spot lay the little bedroom given over to myself and some eighteen or twenty other boys.

The schoolroom was the largest in the house—I could not help thinking, the largest in the world. It was very long, narrow, with painted windows and a low oak ceiling. In one corner was a square of eight or ten feet, bound in by a low wall, where the head of the school sat. Sooner than open the door and enter this place, even when he was away, we would have died the most painful death. In other corners were two other squares, far less feared, but still places of awe. One of these was the seat of the "classical" teacher, the other of the "English and mathematical." Within the room were many benches and desks, black, old, and timeworn, piled with tattered books, and cut with letters, names, and figures, by the knives of boys long since gone. A huge bucket of cold water stood at one end of the room, and a giant clock at the other.

Within the walls of this old school I passed my time during the age of ten to fifteen years, not at all unhappily. The brain of a child needs no outside events to interest it. What might seem a dreary life within these walls, was in truth full of a richer interest and excitement than my later years could ever gain with the aid of wealth, or from crime. The memory of that time is bright and deeply cut.

Yet—from the broader world-view—how little was there to remember! The waking at morning, the nightly call to bed, the hours of study, the classes, the holidays, the walks, the playground with its quarrels, its games, its plotting and trickery. All simple matters—but a magic, now long forgotten, made it a world rich in event and feeling.

I had always been self-willed, and likely to fly out in anger with those who set themselves against me. My parents, from whom I had these traits, did not, or could not, do anything to check the growing evil. Some feeble and unwise efforts on their part failed, and, of course, my self-will grew only the stronger. My voice became the household law, at an age when most children are still guided by the hands of parents.

The warmth of my interests and the force of my will, soon caused me to stand out over all my schoolmates who were not greatly older than I. All except one. He, though we were of no kin, bore the same name as myself, William Wilson. The fact is not strange, for my name, though it had come to me from a noble family, was a common one, often borne by persons of the mob. He alone, among those whom we spoke of as "our set," kept up with me in class work and would not obey my will in the sports and quarrels of the playground.

If there is on earth a despot,[1] it is the master-mind in boyhood who rules the less forceful of his mates. In public I treated Wilson as if I did not fear his power to outdo me. For the way he so easily stood up to me made me feel that he was really in every way the stronger. Since he would not be overcome by me, I must be always straining against him. Yet his strength seemed to be known to no one but myself. Our mates were blind to the struggle between us, for he made no show of the will and force that drove me on to outdo them. In his struggle with me, it seemed that he might have no purpose but to block my will. But there were times when I thought that he showed for me an unwanted liking.

Perhaps it was this liking for me, or the fact of our having the same name, or that it chanced we had entered school on the same day—which started the notion among the older boys that we were brothers. I have said before, that we were not akin. If we had been, we should have been twins, for I learned that he and I had been born on the same day.

In spite of his unbearable manner of setting his will and opinion against mine, I could not bring myself to hate him altogether. Almost every day we quarreled. He might give in to me, but in some way he always made me feel that he, and not I, had been in the right. A sense of pride on my part, and a true worth on his part, kept us always upon what we called "speaking terms." And on many points we agreed so well that we could have become friends, except for this inner struggle. My feelings toward him had something of dislike, more of respect, much of fear, a world of uneasy interest, but not yet any hatred. Needless to say, we were always together.

Most of my attacks upon Wilson were in the form of teasing and practical jokes, in which one can cause pain while seeming to be acting only in fun. But I often failed in this, for his calm manner would not be laughed at. I could

[1] An absolute ruler, usually a tyrant.

find in him but one weak point, which would have been spared by anyone less at wit's end for a means of attack. Whether because of an illness, or a natural fault, his voice could not be raised *above a very low whisper.* I played my jokes upon this weakness of his.

He had many ways of getting even with me. He learned of a petty weakness of mine, and vexed me by playing upon it. He learned that I did not like my very common name, William Wilson. In truth, I hated the sound of the words. And when, upon the day I entered school, a second William Wilson came also, I was vexed because I saw that the use of the name would be doubled in the school, and he would often be mistaken for me, or I for him.

I saw that we were of the same height, and alike in general looks. I was galled, too, by the report that we were brothers. In a word, although I carefully said nothing of my feelings, any mention of us together vexed me greatly. But, in truth, except the story of our being brothers, I think none of our fellows ever thought of any likeness between us. But *he* knew of my fears, for he was keen to see into things. To get even with me, he could vex me by dressing as I did, walking as I did, and otherwise copying my manners. Of course he could not speak as I did, but his whisper *grew to be the very echo of my voice.*

I had one comfort—no one noticed that he was aping me. No one laughed. I had to bear only *his* knowing smiles. He vexed me, too, by an air of having me under his care; he was too ready to advise me. This habit of advising me grew more and more hateful to me as I grew in years. Yet, let me be fair enough to say that never did his advice direct me toward those follies so usual in the young while they still lack worldly wisdom. His moral sense was far keener than my own.

I have said that in the first years that I knew him, I felt a kind of friendship for him. But in the latter months of my stay at the school, what I began to feel for him was very like hate. He saw this, I think, and began to keep away from me, or to make a show of doing so. Once, about this time, we had an open quarrel. He was thrown quite off his guard, and spoke more openly of my failings than usual. At that moment a wild idea came to my mind that I had known him before. In his manner and in his looks, I saw, or thought I saw something that startled me by bringing to mind dim visions of my earliest childhood—when memory itself was yet unborn. But the feeling passed away. I mention it only because that was the last day I talked with him.

Wilson had a small room—or rather closet—where he slept by himself. One night near the close of my fifth year at school, and just after the quarrel, I got up, took a lamp, and stole through the narrow passages to his bedroom. My purpose was to play him one of my ill-natured practical jokes. L left the lamp with a shade over it, outside his room, while I went in and listened to his breathing until I knew that he was asleep. Then I brought in the shaded lamp, went up to his bed, and drew back the curtains.

The lamplight fell upon his sleeping face. As I looked, an icy chill ran through my body. I bent still closer over the face. Was it the face of William Wilson? Not thus did he look in his lively waking hours. The same name! The same figure! Coming to school the same day as I! And then his dogged copy of my walk, my voice, my habits, and my manner! Was *what I now saw* the result of his aping my ways? Awestruck and with a creeping shudder, I put out the lamp and silently stole from his room. Next day I left the halls of the old school, never to enter them again.

After some months, spent at home in idleness, I became a student at Eton. There I plunged into a life of thoughtless folly. I do not wish to trace the full course of my life there. Three years passed with nothing gained but habits of vice, and inches added to my height.

One evening I asked a small party of students, with habits like my own, to a drunken revel in my rooms. The meeting lasted all night, and wine flowed freely. Gray dawn was in the east when my servant came to say that someone in great haste wished to speak with me outside. I staggered out into the hall. In this small room, there being no lamp, the only light was that of the feeble dawn which came through a small window. There stood a young man, about my own height, dressed in the same novel fashion that I followed at the moment. In the faint light, I could not see his face, but he came up to me, took me angrily by the arm, and whispered in my ear, "William Wilson."

I was sober in a moment. Something in his manner, in the shake of his finger uplifted between me and the dim window, filled me with awe. Before I could collect my senses, he was gone.

I did not deny to myself that I knew who the strange visitor had been. But who and what was this Wilson? Where had he come from? Why had he come? For some weeks I tried to learn something of him. I learned only that because of an accident in his family, he had left the old school on the same afternoon that I ran away from it. But in a short time I ceased to think upon the subject, my attention being taken up in preparing to leave for Oxford, where I soon went.

My parents' pride caused them to set me up with money enough to live on a plane with sons of the richest earls in Great Britain. But as I kept to my old ways of folly and vice, the money they gave me was not enough. It is hard to believe, but I sank so low as to go among gamblers to learn their vile arts, which I used against weak-minded fellow students. This I did in order to add to the already large income given me by my parents.

For some time I took money from them while still holding my old place in the society of my fellows. Who—even among those as wild as I—would believe evil the gay, the frank, the free-spending William Wilson! Ah, no—his folly was but the wildness of youth, his vices but the careless, dashing ways of a young man.

I had been two years a gambler, when there came to the college a wealthy young man named Glendenning—*very* wealthy, it was said, and easily duped. Of course I marked him as one fit for me to try my skill on. I played cards with him often, and at first let him win large sums from me. I met him one evening at the rooms of Preston, a fellow student, who knew nothing of my plans. Eight or ten others were there. If I chose this time to win large sums from Glendenning, no one would ever think I had planned it. So, I acted at first as if I did not wish to play that evening. But the game being started, we played far into the night.

At last I managed to get Glendenning into a game with me alone. The rest of the company watched. Glendenning, whom I had led to drink heavily, played in a wild, nervous manner. He soon owed me a large sum. Suddenly, as I had hoped he would, he offered to double the stakes. Again I acted as if I did not wish to do this, but at last I agreed. In less than an hour, he owed me four times the sum. He grew very pale, and I soon learned that the sum I had won from him was all he had. He was ruined. A gloomy silence fell over all, and I felt my cheeks tingle from the burning glances of scorn cast upon me by those who pitied Glendenning.

At this moment, the folding doors of the room were suddenly thrown wide open, with a rush of air that blew out every candle there. We had only a glimpse of a man who entered, a man about my own height.

"Gentlemen," he said in a low and never-to-be forgotten *whisper,* which thrilled to the very marrow of my bones, "you do not know the nature of the person who has just won a large sum of money from Glendenning. Look at the lining of his left sleeve, and at the several little packages which may be found in his pockets."

He left the room at once. In the stillness that followed, one might have heard a pin drop upon the floor. Then many hands roughly took hold of me, and the candles were re-lighted. In the lining of my sleeve, and in my pockets were found cards, as the stranger had said. The silent scorn that followed was harder to bear than a burst of anger would have been.

"Mr. Wilson," said our host, stooping to pick up my cloak of rare furs, "this is yours. I hope you will see the need to leave Oxford at once—in any case, to leave my rooms."

Shamed to the dust as I then was, it is likely I should have met his words with blows, if I had not been shocked to see the cloak he was holding out to me. My own cloak was already on my arm. The stranger who had come and gone must have left the cloak that Preston held. It too was made of rare furs, like my own. I took it and placed it, unnoticed, over my own, and left with an angry face. The next morning before dawn, I left Oxford and fled to Paris, in an agony of shame.

I fled in vain. Scarcely had I set foot in Paris when I had proof of Wilson's hated interest in me. Years flew, and all the while I was never free of him. At Rome, he stepped in between me and my hopes, between me and my revenge at Vienna, between me and my great love at Naples, between me and my gain in Egypt. Where, in truth, did I *not* have bitter cause to curse him in my heart? I fled from him to the very ends of the earth. *I fled in vain.*

Again and again I asked myself, "Who is he? where does he come from? what is his purpose?" But I found no answer. I began to study the forms and methods of his attacks on me. But I learned little that would help me answer the questions. I did notice that he crossed my path only to prevent my carrying out plans that would cause bitter harm. But this was a poor excuse for taking away my natural right to lead my own life in my own way.

At last I told myself that I would no longer bear this. Since our school days, he had never let me see his face, but I knew him all the same. One evening, when I was at a masked ball in Rome, and had drunk too much wine, I felt a light hand placed on my shoulder, and heard that low, hated whisper in my ear. In fury I turned upon him. As usual the clothes he wore were the same as mine. This time it was a Spanish cloak of blue velvet, with a broad red sash holding a sword. A mask of black silk covered his face.

"Scoundrel!" I said in a voice husky with rage, "you *shall not* dog me to death! Follow me, or I will stab you where you stand!"

I pushed my way from the ballroom into a small room near by, dragging him with me. Upon entering this room, I thrust him from me with such force that he staggered against the wall. I first turned to close the door, then faced him and with an oath told him to draw his sword. He paused a moment, then with a slight sigh, drew his sword and took his place before me.

The duel was soon over. I was wild with anger, and felt in my arm the power of many men. In a few seconds I had forced him to the wall, had him at my mercy, and plunged my sword through his body again and again. At that moment somebody tried the latch of the door. I hurried to make sure it was locked, and then turned back to my dying foe.

William Wilson

But in that moment when my eyes were turned away from him, a change had come over the place. Now a large mirror—so at first it seemed to me—stood where I had not seen one before. In it I saw my own image, with pale face and dabbled in blood. It moved to meet me with tottering steps. So it *seemed*, I say, but was not. It was my foe—it was Wilson, who stood before me in the agony of death. His mask and cloak lay where he had thrown them upon the floor. Not a thread in all his clothes—not a line in all his face which was not *my own!*

It was Wilson, but he spoke no longer in a whisper. I could have fancied that I myself was speaking while he said:

"You have won and I give up. Yet from now on, you are also dead—dead to the World—to Heaven—to Hope! In me did you live—and in my death, see by this image, which is your own, how utterly you have murdered yourself!"

HUMOROUS STORIES

Never Bet the Devil Your Head

Three Sundays in a Week

The System of Dr. Tarr
and Prof. Fether

The Spectacles

Never Bet the Devil Your Head

I do not wish to speak ill of my poor friend Toby. He had sad faults, and he died a sad death. But he himself was not to blame for his vices. His mother did her best for him, while he was small, in the way of flogging him. She thought that small boys were like tough steaks, the better for beating. But, poor woman, she was left-handed, and it is worse for a child to be flogged left-handed than not to be flogged at all. The world turns from right to left, and it will not do to whip a child from left to right. If each blow in the proper direction drives an evil out, then every thump in the other direction must surely drive a wickedness in. I often stood by when Toby was being punished, and I could see, even by the way he kicked, that he was getting worse and worse every day. At last, I saw, through tears in my eyes, that there was no hope for him at all.

One day, he had been cuffed until he grew so black in the face that he looked like a little African. But the only effect was to cause him to wriggle himself into a fit. That day I lifted up my voice and foretold that he would never come to any good end.

The fact is, he was always way ahead of his years, in vice. At five months of age, he would go into such fits of rage that he could not speak. At six months, I caught him biting on a pack of cards. At eight months, he would not sign the pledge never to drink. Thus he went on, growing in vice, month after month, until by the end of his first year he was cursing and swearing, and backing up what he said by betting his head.

It was through this vice of betting, that the ruin which I had foretold for Toby overtook him at last. His habit of betting had grown as he grew, so that when he came to be a man, he could hardly speak a sentence without offering to bet on it.

Not that he really *laid* wagers—no. I will do him the justice to say that he would as soon have laid eggs. With him the thing was a mere habit—nothing more. His bets had no meaning whatever. They were simply words used to round off a sentence. When he said, "I'll bet you so and so," nobody ever thought of taking him up. Still, I could not help thinking it my duty to warn him. Betting was a bad habit, I told him; it was a vulgar habit, and society frowned upon it. But he only smiled. I begged—he laughed. I preached—he sneered. I threatened—he swore. I kicked him—and he offered to bet the devil his head that I would not try that again.

He was very poor, and this was the reason, no doubt, that he never bet money. I never heard him say, "I'll bet you a dollar." He would say instead, "I'll bet you what you please." Or, "I'll bet you what you dare." Or, "I'll bet you a trifle." Or—of less value still—"I'll bet the devil my head."

If he had been taken up on the last bet and had lost, his loss would have been small, for his head was small. He grew so fond of this wager that at last he never made any other but "I'll bet the devil my head."

Once more I vowed to turn him from the habit, if I could. I gathered up all my force, and gave him a last, long talk, trying to get him to overcome this vice. When I had finished my long speech, Toby kept silent for some moments, merely looking me straight in the face. Then he threw his head to one side and raised his eyebrows as high as he could. Then he spread out his hands, palms up, and shrugged his soulders. Then he winked, first his right eye, next his left. Then he opened both eyes so wide that I was afraid of what might happen to him. Then he put his thumb to his nose and waggled his fingers. Finally he settled his hands on his hips and spoke.

I cannot remember all that he said. But he would thank me to hold my tongue. He wished none of my advice. He was old enough to take care of himself. Did I still think he was a baby? Was I trying to insult him? Was I a fool? Did my mother know I was away from home? These questions he put to me, he said, as to a man of truth, and he would believe my answer. And once more, he would ask me plainly, *did* my mother know that I was out. He would be willing, he said, to bet the devil his head that she did not.

He did not wait for my answer, but turned and left in great haste. It was well for him that he did so. My feelings had been hurt. Even my anger had been aroused. For once, I would have taken him up on his bet. He would have lost, for my mama *did* know that I had left home to be gone a short time. But I had brought the insult on myself in doing my duty, and I bore it like a man.

It now seemed that I had done for him all that could be expected of me. I made up my mind to trouble him no more with my advice, but to leave him to his evil talk. But I could not bring myself to give up seeing him altogether.

One fine day we strolled out together, arm in arm. Toby was in high spirits. He made quite a tomfool of himself. He went skipping over and wriggling under everything that came in his way, now shouting out and now lisping out all kinds of odd words, little and big, and yet keeping the straightest face in the world, all the time. I really could not make up my mind whether I ought to kick him or to pity him. Our way led over a river, which we crossed on a covered bridge. To protect it from the weather, the bridge had been not only roofed over, but also walled in, and as there were few windows, the walk across was quite dark. The gloom caused my spirits to sink, but Toby was gay as ever.

When we were nearly across the bridge, we came to a turn-stile of some height. I passed quietly through, pushing it around as usual. But this ordinary way of going through a turnstile would not do for the gay Toby. He would jump over it—he said he could do it and cut a pigeonwing[1] in the air over it.

Now, I did not think he could, and I told him, in so many words, that he was a braggart and could not do what he said. For saying this, I had reason to be sorry afterward. For he at once offered *to bet the devil his head* that he could. Just as he said the words, I heard, close at my elbow, a slight cough—"Ahem!"

I started, and looked around in surprise. There, in a nook made by the framework of the bridge, was a little, lame old gentleman. He looked like a kindly well-meaning old fellow, and was dressed in a black suit and a clean shirt with the collar turned very neatly down over a white tie. His hair was parted in the middle like a girl's. He stood quietly, his hands resting together over his stomach, his two eyes rolled up. Looking at him more closely, I saw that he wore a black silk apron, and this was a thing which I thought very odd.

"Toby," I said, "the old gentleman says 'Ahem.' "

Now, even I did not think this remark of mine showed any great wisdom. But if I had dealt Toby a stunning blow, he would hardly have been more moved than by my simple words. (I have often noticed that what we say to others may not have the effect that we look for.)

"You don't say so," he gasped, turning from one color to another. "Are you quite sure he said *that?* Well, I am in for it now, and may as well go through with it. Here goes, then—*Ahem!*"

At this, the old gentleman seemed pleased. He left his place in the nook of the bridge, limped forward, took Toby by the hand, and shook it warmly.

---

[1] A fancy step, in skating or dancing, made by jumping and striking the legs together.

"I am quite sure you will win," he said with a frank smile, "but we must make the trial, you know, for the sake of mere form."

"Ahem!" said Toby, taking off his coat, with a deep sigh, and turning up his eyes and bringing down the corners of his mouth till he looked like an old sheep lost in thought.

The old gentleman now took him by the arm, and led him more into the shade of the bridge, a few steps back from the turnstile, saying:

"I wish to be fair with you, and so will allow you this much run. Now, wait here until I take my place by the stile, so that I may see whether you go over it well, and don't leave out the pigeonwing. I will say 'One, two, three, and away.' You are to start at the word *away*."

He went and took his place by the stile, paused a moment as if in deep thought, then *looked up* and, I thought, smiled very slightly. He tightened the strings of his apron, took a long look at Toby, and at last gave the words, "One—two—three—and away!"

At the word *away* my poor friend set off in a strong gallop. The stile was not so high and I thought that he would be able to clear it. But what if he did not?

"What right," thought I, "has the old gentleman to make him jump? Who is *he*? If he asks *me* to jump, I won't do it, that's flat, and I don't care who *the devil he is.*"

The bridge was so walled in, that there was an echo in it at all times—but I had not heard it so plainly as when I spoke those last words. But no matter. My poor Toby was taking the leap. I saw him run nimbly, and spring grandly from the floor of the bridge, cutting the most awful flourishes with his legs as he went up. I saw him high in the air, pigeonwinging his way just over the top of the stile. But what was so strange was that he did not *go on over,* but down he came on the flat of his back, on the same side of the stile that he had started on. At the same moment, I saw the old gentleman go limping off at the top of his speed, having caught and wrapped up in his apron some object that fell heavily into it from the darkness of the arched bridge just over the stile.

Toby lay there very still. I thought that his feelings had been hurt by his failure, and that he needed me. I hurried up to him, and saw that he had what I might call a serious hurt. The truth is, his head was gone. And after a close search all about, I could not find it anywhere. I made up my mind I had better take him home as he was, and send for the doctors at once. Then a thought struck me. I threw open a window of the bridge to let in more light, and the sad truth flashed upon me at once.

In the added light, I saw, about five feet above the top of the turnstile, a flat iron bar, a brace, running from one side of the bridge to the other. It was plain that the edge of this brace had struck upon the neck of my poor friend Toby.

He did not live long after his terrible loss. The medicine which the doctors would have given him, he could not take. So he grew worse and worse, and at last died, a lesson to all evil talkers.

Three Sundays in a Week

"**Y**ou hard-headed, stubborn, crusty, old savage!" said I, in fancy, one afternoon to my great-uncle. I shook my fist at him—also in fancy. Only in fancy. There was indeed quite a difference between what I said and what I wished to say—between what I did and what I had half a mind to do.

The old wretch, as I opened the dining room door, was sitting with his feet upon the mantelpiece, holding a glass of wine in his paw, and making a great try at singing a ditty.

"My *dear* uncle," I said, closing the door gently, and going up to him with the blandest of smiles, "you are always so kind and thoughtful—that—that—I know I have only to bring up this little matter once more, and you will do as we wish."

"Hem!" he said. "Good boy! Go on."

"I am sure, my dearest uncle" (you old rascal) "that you really have no wish to keep me from marrying Kate. Your holding out against us is merely a joke of yours, I know—ha! ha! ha!—you are so full of jokes!"

"Ha! ha! ha!" he laughed. "Yes, yes, full of fun."

"To be sure—of course! I *knew* you were joking. Now, uncle, all that Kate and I ask at this time, is that you tell us what *day* will suit you best for the wedding to—to come off, you know."

"To come off! What do you mean by that? Better wait till it goes on."

"Ha! ha! ha! Oh, that is good! You are such a wit! But all

we want just now, uncle, is that you name the day—any day—any *certain* day."

"Ah—name the day, eh?"

"Yes, uncle—any day that you like."

"Well, Bobby, won't it do to say—sometime within a year or so—must I name a *certain* day."

"If you please, uncle, a certain day."

"Well, then, Bobby, my boy, since you *will* have a certain day, I will do as you ask for once."

"Dear uncle—"

"Hush, sir!" he cried, drowning out my voice. "I will do as you ask for once. You shall have Kate—and her fortune—let me see—when shall it be? Today is Sunday, isn't it? Well, then, you shall be married—now mind!—*when three Sundays come together in a week!* Do you hear me, sir? What are you staring at? I say you shall have Kate and her fortune when three Sundays come together in a week—but not *till* then, not if I die for it. You know me—*I am a man of my word*—now be off!"

Here he drank his glass of wine, while I rushed from the room.

My great-uncle was a little somebody, with a red nose, a thick skull, a long purse, and a strong will. He liked to hold out against the wishes of others. To every question, a firm "No!" was his quick reply. But in the end—in the long, long end—he usually gave way. He was most stubborn in saying "No!" when anyone asked him for money. But the amount of money that he gave at last, was generally more than had been first asked for.

I had lived with the old gentleman all my life. My parents, in dying, had left me to him, as a rich gift. I believe the old villain loved me as his own child—nearly if not quite as well as he loved Kate. But it was a dog's life that he led me. From the time I was one year old until I was five, he flogged me every day. From the age of five to fifteen, I heard daily that I was on the highroad to the reform school. From the age of fifteen to twenty, not a day passed that I did not hear a threat of being left out of his will.

In Kate, however, I had a firm friend. She told me sweetly that I might have her, fortune and all, whenever I could get my great-uncle to say "Yes" to the wedding. Poor girl! She was very young, and her wealth would be tied up for five more years. What, then, to do? When one is young, five years seem like five hundred years.

In vain we pleaded with the old gentleman. Here was a chance for him to say "No," a chance which suited him to a T. It would have made even a saint angry to see how like an old mouser he acted toward us two poor little mice. In his heart, he wished above all things to see us wed. He had his mind fixed on this all along. In fact, he would have given ten thousand from his own pocket (Kate's fortune was her own, coming from her mother), if he could have seen us wed without having to say "Yes" to our wishes.

After his own fashion, he was a man of his word, beyond a doubt. This keeping his word to the letter was, in fact, one of his hobbies. He could break the *spirit* of a promise, but the *letter* of his word, he always kept. Now, it was to the *letter of his word* that Kate very cleverly held him, one fine day, not long after my talk with him. It came about this way.

It happened that two naval officers, friends of ours, had just come back to London after a year of travel around the world. With these two to help us, Kate and I made a plan. As it was planned, they came together to visit my great-uncle on Sunday afternoon, October 10. For half an hour, we talked about this and that. At last Captain Pratt said to my uncle:

"Well, I have been away just one year. This is October 10. You will remember, my dear sir, that I called her October 10, a year ago, to say good-bye."

"Yes, yes," said my uncle, "I remember it very well."

"It is rather strange," said Capain Smitherton, "but I too have been away just one year today. You will remember

that I too called that same day last year, to say good-bye."

"That is true," said my uncle. "Very queer—both of you gone just one year to a day."

"But remember, my dear sir," broke in Kate, "they did not travel in the same direction. That makes a difference, you know. Captain Pratt went round Cape Horn, and Captain Smitherton went round the Cape of Good Hope."

"Of course," said my uncle, "one went east and the other went west, you silly girl. But that makes no difference. They both went around the world, didn't they?"

"You must both come and spend the evening with us tomorrow," I said. "Then you can tell us all about your trip, and we shall have a game of cards—"

"Cards, my dear fellow," said Pratt. "You forget that tomorrow will be Sunday. Some other evening—"

"Why, shame on you, Captain Pratt!" cried Kate. "*Today* is Sunday!"

"To be sure," said my uncle, "today is Sunday."

"I beg your pardon," said Pratt, "but I cannot be so much mistaken. I know that tomorrow is Sunday, because—"

Here Smitherton broke in. "What *are* you all thinking about! *Yesterday* was Sunday!"

"*Today* is Sunday," said my uncle, in a loud voice. "Don't I know?"

"I see it!" cried Kate, jumping up eagerly. "We are *all* right. Captain Pratt says tomorrow will be Sunday. So it will be—for him. Captain Smitherton says that yesterday was Sunday. So it was—for him. And thus *three Sundays have come together in a week!*"

"Kate is right," said Smitherton, after a pause. "Captain Pratt, what fools we two are! The matter is thus," he said, turning to my uncle. "The earth, as you know, is a little more than twenty-four thousand miles around. We will say it is an even twenty-four thousand miles around. It spins from west to east in twenty-four hours. That is at a rate of a thousand miles an hour. Now, when I had sailed from London a thousand miles east, I saw the sun rise one hour sooner than you here in London. Going on another thousand miles, I saw the sun rise two hours sooner than you here in London. And so on, until I went around the globe and back to London. Having gone twenty-four thousand miles, I have seen the sun rise a total of twenty-four hours ahead of its rise in London. That is to say, I am a day *ahead* of your time.

Thus, yesterday was Sunday to me."

"Oh, yes," said my uncle, "of course, but—"

Captain Smitherton raised his voice over my uncle's and went on speaking. "Captain Pratt, on the other hand, went west. When he had sailed a thousand miles west of London, he was an hour *behind* the time in London, for he saw the sun rise an hour later than you did here. When he had sailed twenty-four thousand miles, and was back in London, he was twenty-four hours behind the time of London. Thus, to Pratt, tomorrow is Sunday. And what is more, dear sir, we are *all* right—yesterday was Sunday to me. Today is Sunday to you. Tomorrow will be Sunday to Pratt!"

"Well, Kate," said my uncle, "well, Bobby, I am a man of my word—*notice that!* You shall be married when you please. Done up, by Jove! Three Sundays all in a row!"

The System of Dr. Tarr and Prof. Fether

One fine day, while I was traveling in the south of France, I passed within a few miles of a private madhouse. I had heard much about this place, from my medical friends in Paris, and I thought I should not miss the chance to see it.

I spoke of this to my traveling companion, a gentleman whom I had learned to know while in this part of France. But he did not wish to visit the place; he did not have time, and he felt a horror at the sight of a lunatic. He would not, however, stand in the way of my going. He would ride ahead, and I could overtake him the next day, if not that day. I said that perhaps I would not be allowed to enter the place.

"Indeed," he said, "unless you have letters to Superintendent Maillard, it is likely that you will not. Private madhouses, such as this, are very strict in their rules."

He went on to say that he had met Superintendent Maillard some years ago, and that he would ride with me up to the door, and make me known to him.

I thanked him and we turned from the main road into a grass-grown by-path, which soon nearly lost itself in a forest. Through this wood we rode some two miles, before the madhouse came in sight. It was a large old place, that showed age and some lack of care.

As we rode up to the gateway, I saw the gate open slightly, and a man's face peered through. The next moment, he came out and greeted my companion by name, shook his hand, and asked us to come in. It was Superintendent Maillard himself, a portly, fine-looking gentleman, with a polite manner and an air of grave command.

My friend told him of my wish to see the place, and Superintendent Maillard said he would be pleased to show it to me. My friend then took leave and rode on.

The superintendent led me into a small neat parlor, where there were books, pictures, flowers, and a cheerful fire blazing on the hearth. A very beautiful young lady sat at a piano singing. She paused in her song as we came in, and gave me a graceful welcome. Her voice was low, and her whole manner gentle and quiet. I thought her face rather sad, and she seemed pale. She was dressed in deep mourning.

I had heard at Paris that this place was managed by Superintendent Maillard upon what was called the "system of soothing." That is, the patients were treated, as far as possible, like persons in their right minds. They were left free to roam about the house and grounds, though of course they were secretly watched. Knowing this, I was careful what I said before the young lady, for I could not be sure that she was sane. In fact, there was a too bright look in her eyes which half led me to think that she was not. I spoke, therefore, of everyday matters, such as I thought would not excite even a lunatic. She replied in a very sane manner to all that I said. But I was a medical student, and I knew that a lunatic may at times seem to be quite sane.

After a while, a smartly dressed footman brought in a tray with fruit and wine. Soon after, the lady left the room. As she went out, I looked at Superintendent Maillard with a question in my eyes.

"No," he said, "oh no—one of my own family—my niece, and a very talented woman."

"I beg a thousand pardons for the thought!" I said. "But

at Paris we know of your method here, and I thought she might be—you know—"

"Yes, yes, say no more. In fact, you are quite right to act with caution. A thoughtless visitor here can be, and often has been, the cause of trouble. While my former system was in force here, and my patients went about at will, they were sometimes thrown into a frenzy, by some act of a person who had come to see the place. So, I have had to be careful that no visitor is brought in, whom I do not know."

"While your *former* system was in force!" I said. "Am I to understand that the *soothing system,* of which I have heard so much, is no longer in force?"

"We had to give it up," he said, "several weeks ago."

"Indeed! You surprise me."

"Yes," he said, with a sigh, "the *danger* of the soothing system was too great. What we gained by it was not enough to justify the danger. We gave it a fair trial—but it would not work. I am sorry you did not visit us earlier, so you might have seen the system in force, and have judged for yourself. I believe that you know the nature of the soothing system?"

"Not altogether. What I have heard has been at third or fourth hand."

"In general, it was this. We never set ourselves against the patient. No matter what fancy entered his mad brain, we acted as if we thought he was right. Many great cures were brought about in this way. For you cannot reason with a madman, but you can lead him to see that his idea is wrong, by helping him to carry it out. We have had men who fancied themselves to be chickens. The cure was to act as if they were chickens in fact, and to give them nothing to eat but chicken feed. A few days on a diet of corn and gravel may do wonders to take away the false idea."

"And this was your sole method of treatment?"

"By no means. We kept them busy and interested, with music, dancing, and other exercises, cards, and certain kinds of books. The words *lunatic, madman, crazy person* were never spoken. Another point was to set each lunatic to guard all the others. To put faith in a madman is to win him body and soul."

"And you never locked them up?"

"Very rarely. Now and then, one would take a sudden turn of fury, and we would have to take him to a cell. We kept him there until we could send him back to his family or friends, for with the raging lunatic we have nothing to do."

"And you have now given up this system—and you think for the better?"

"Yes. As I said, dangers of the system proved to be too great. And there were other faults to it. After dinner I will be happy to take you over the house and show you our system now in use, which, I believe, is the best that has ever yet been used."

"Another of your own ideas?"

"I am proud to say it is—at least, in part—my idea. But we will wait until after dinner. There is always something more or less of a shock in the sight of lunatics, and I would not spoil your dinner."

At six o'clock dinner was announced. Superintendent Maillard led me into a large dining room, where we found twenty-five or thirty people. They seemed to be persons of rank—certainly of good breeding. Of the ladies, some were dressed in very good taste, in the latest fashion. But others— some of them not less than seventy years old—showed a taste for too much finery, and were decked with rings, brace- lets, earrings, and wore their bosoms and arms shamefully bare. I noticed, too, that many of them wore poorly-made dresses.

Looking about, I saw the girl whom I had met in the little parlor. What was my surprise to see her dressed up in a hoop skirt, high-heeled shoes, and a dirty lace cap much too large for her. She had been dressed, when I had first seen her, very neatly, in deep mourning.

In short, there was something so very odd about the dress

of the whole party that for the moment I went back to my first thought, that I was seeing the soothing system at work. Maillard, I thought, may have been keeping me in the dark until after dinner, fearing I might not enjoy eating if I knew I was in the company of lunatics. But I remembered having been told in Paris that the people of southern France tend to be rather odd, each one going along in his own old-fashioned way. Then, too, after talking with several of the company, any idea that they were a body of lunatics left me.

The dining room was large, but very bare, no carpet on the floor, no curtains at the windows, which were made fast with iron bars. But the table was well set with shining silver, and loaded down with rich food. Never in my life had I seen such a wasteful amount of good things to eat.

153

Dinner was not served in the best of taste. My eyes, used to quiet lights, met the glare of many wax candles, which in their silver holders were set upon the table and all about the room wherever a place could be found. Several servants moved quickly about, and upon a large table at the farther end of the room were seated seven or eight people with fiddles, fifes, trombones, and a drum. From time to time during the dinner, these gave forth with a great noise, which was not music, but which seemed to please everyone but myself.

Upon the whole, I could not help thinking that there was much that was strange about everything that I saw—but then the world is made up of all kinds of people, with all kinds of customs.

During dinner, the talk was lively and general. The ladies, as usual, talked a great deal. I soon found that nearly all of the company were well educated. Maillard had a world of good-humored talk himself. He seemed quite willing to speak of his work as superintendent there. Indeed, the topic of lunacy was, much to my surprise, a favorite one with all of them. Many good stories were told about the whims of the patients.

"We had a fellow here once," said a fat little gentleman, who sat at my right, "that fancied himself to be a silver teapot, and was very careful to polish himself every morning."

"And then," said a tall man, across the table, "we had not long ago, a person who had taken it into his head that he was a donkey—which you might say was very true. He gave us trouble. We could hardly keep him within bounds. For a long time he would eat nothing but thistles. But we cured him of the idea by giving him nothing else to eat. Then he was always kicking out his heels—like this—"

"Mr. DeKock! I will thank you to behave yourself," broke in an old lady, who sat beside him. "Please keep your feet to yourself! You have spoiled my dress. Can't you tell a story without acting it?"

"A thousand pardons, Madame Laplace." He bowed low and kissed his hand with much ceremony.

"And then," said a thin-looking person near the foot of the table, "we had a patient once who said he was a cheese, and went around with a knife in his hand, urging his friends to try a small slice from the middle of his leg."

"He was a great fool," said another, "but not as funny as the one who took himself for a bottle of champagne, and always went off with a pop and a fizz, like this—"

Here the speaker, very rudely, as I thought, put his right thumb into his left cheek, withdrew it with a sound like the popping of a cork, then by blowing between his tongue and his teeth made a sharp hissing and fizzing that lasted several minutes, like the frothing of champagne. This act, I saw plainly, was not very pleasing to Maillard, but he said nothing.

The storytelling was picked up by a very lean little man in a big wig. "And then there was the one who thought himself a frog, and he really did look like one. I wish you could have seen him, sir"—here he turned to speak to me—"sir, if that man was *not* a frog, I can only say it was a pity he was not. His croak, like this—o-o-o-o-gh—o-o-o-o-gh! was the finest note in the world—B-flat. And when he put his elbows upon the table, like this—after taking a glass or two of wine—and opened his mouth wide, like this—and rolled up his eyes, like this—and winked them very fast, this way—why, then, sir, you would have said he was a man of genius."

"No doubt," I said.

"And then," said somebody else, "there was the one who thought himself a pinch of snuff, and kept trying to take himself up between his own finger and thumb."

"And then there was Jules, who went mad with the idea that he was a pumpkin. He begged the cook to make him up into pies—which the cook wouldn't do. But for my part, I am not so sure that a pumpkin pie á la Jules would not have been very good eating!"

I began to wonder more and more, and looked at Maillard. He laughed and said:

"Our friend here is a wit—you must not think he means everything he says."

"And then," said someone of the party, "there was that big fellow, that went mad for love and fancied he had two heads. He could have been wrong, but he could make you think he was right, for he was a fine speaker. He used to jump up on the dinner table, just like this—"

Here a friend at his side put a hand upon his shoulder and whispered a few low words in his ear, upon which he suddenly stopped talking and sank back in his chair.

"And then," said the one who had whispered to quiet the other, "there was the top. I call him the top because he had taken a queer fancy that he was a top. You would have roared with laughter to see him spin. He would turn round upon one heel by the hour—this way—"

Here the friend whom he had quieted, did the same for him in return.

"But then," cried an old lady, at the top of her voice, "he was nothing but a madman, and a very silly one at best. Who ever heard of a human top? The thing is silly. Madame Joyeuse was a more sensible person, as you know. She had a fancy too, but it was full of good sense and gave pleasure to all who had the honor to know her. She found that she had been turned into a rooster, but, as such, she behaved properly. She flapped her wings with great skill—this way— like this! And, as for her crow, it was beautiful! Cock-a-doodle-doo! Cock-a-doodle-doo! Cock-a-doodle-de-doo-doo-dooo-do-o-o-o-o-o-!"

"Madame Joyeuse," here Maillard called out, very angry, "you can either act as a lady should, or you can leave the table at once—take your choice."

The lady (whom I was much surprised to hear called Madame Joyeuse, after what she herself had just said of Madame Joyeuse) blushed up to her eyebrows, hung down her head, and said not a word in reply. But another and younger lady took up the matter. It was my beautiful girl of the little parlor!

"Oh, Madame Joyeuse *was* a fool," she cried, "but there was really much sound sense in Eugénie Salsafette. She was a beautiful young lady, and very modest. She said the usual way of dressing the body was all wrong, not modest. She wished to dress herself by getting outside, instead of inside her clothes. It is very easily done. You have only to do this—and this—and then—"

"Good heavens! Madame Salsafette," cried a dozen voices at once. "What *are* you doing? Stop! That is enough! We see how it is done! Stop! Stop!"

Several persons were already jumping up to stop her, when we were all brought to a stand by hearing loud screams or yells coming from somewhere in the building.

My own nerves were shaken by these yells, but the rest of the company I really pitied. They grew pale as so many corpses, and sinking back in their chairs, sat trembling and chattering with terror. I asked Maillard what was the cause of the screams.

"Oh nothing," he said. "We are used to these things. The lunatics every now and then start to howling all at once. One starts another, as dogs sometimes do at night. Sometimes the howling ends in a mob rush to break loose. Then, of course, there is a little danger."

"And how many patients have you here?"

"At this time, not more than ten."

"Chiefly women, I suppose?"

"Oh, no—every one of them men, and strong fellows, too, I can tell you. Some time ago there were twenty-seven patients here, and eighteen of them were women. But lately matters have changed."

"Yes—have changed very much, as you see," said DeKock.

"Yes—have changed very much, as you see!" chimed in the whole company at once.

"Hold your tongues, every one of you!" cried Maillard, in a great rage.

The whole company was silent for nearly a minute.

"And this lady," I said to Maillard in a whisper—"this good lady who gives the cock-a-doodle-de-do—she is quite harmless, eh?"

"Harmless!" he cried in real surprise, "why—why, what *can* you mean?"

"She is only slightly touched?" I said, tapping my forehead.

"Good heavens! What *are* you thinking of? This lady, my very old friend, Madame Joyeuse, is as sane as I am. She has her little odd ways, to be sure—but then, you know, some old people do become more or less odd."

"To be sure," I said. "And then the rest of these people—"

"Are my friends and helpers," said Superintendent Maillard, drawing himself up with pride, "my very good friends and helpers."

"What! All of them? The women and all?"

"Of course," he said. "We could not do at all without the women. They are the best lunatic nurses in the world."

"To be sure," I said "By the way, did I understand that the new system used here now—in place of your well-known soothing system—is a very harsh one?"

"By no means. We put them under lock and key now, but the medical treatment is rather pleasant than otherwise."

"And this new system is one of your own ideas?"

"Not altogether. Parts of it we took from Doctor Tarr, whom you know, of course. And some of the plan, I am happy to say, belongs by right to the great Professor Fether, whom you must know."

"I am ashamed to say that I have never heard of either," I said.

"Good heavens!" he said, lifting his hands, "you never *heard* of the learned Doctor Tarr, or of the famous Professor Fether?"

"I am humbled to the dust. I will seek out their writings at once. You have *really* made me ashamed of myself." And this was the fact.

"Say no more, my good friend," he said kindly. "Join me now in a glass of wine."

We drank. The company joined us without stint. They chatted. They jested. They laughed. They did a thousand silly tricks. The fiddles shrieked. The drum row-de-dowed. The trombone bellowed. And the whole place became more and more like a madhouse every minute.

In the meantime, Maillard and I talked at the top of our voices. A word spoken in an ordinary tone stood no more chance of being heard than the voice of a fish from the bottom of Niagara Falls.

"And, sir," I screamed in his ear, "you believe the old soothing system was one of danger?"

"Yes," he said, "there was sometimes great danger. There is no way of knowing what a madman may take into his head to do. I believe—and Doctor Tarr and Professor Fether agree—that is it *never* safe to let them run at large. A lunatic may be soothed, as it is called, for a time, but, in the end, he is apt to give trouble. He is cunning, too. When he is planning something, he is very clever at hiding his plans. And the way that he can act like a sane man, is one of the strangest puzzles in our study of the mind. When a madman seems *thoroughly* sane, it is high time to put him in a straitjacket."

"But did you ever—in your work here—meet with danger?"

"Here? Why, I may say, yes. Not *very* long ago, a strange thing happened in this very house. The soothing system was then in use, and the patients were free to come and go. They behaved very well—so very well that one of sense might have known that something was brewing. And, sure enough, one fine morning, they turned in a body against the keepers, bound them hand and foot, and locked them in the cells as if *they* were the lunatics. The lunatics themselves became the keepers."

"You don't tell me so! I never heard of anything so odd in my life!"

"Fact—it all came to pass by means of a stupid fellow—a lunatic—who had taken it into his head that he had a better system of caring for lunatics than had ever been heard of. He wished to give his system a trial, and so he got the rest of the patients to join with him and overthrow the true keepers."

"But how long did this overthrow hold out—not long, of course. People in this region—visitors—would give the alarm."

"There you are wrong. The head rebel was a cunning fellow. He didn't allow any visitors at all—except one, a very stupid-looking young man who came one day to see the place. He let him in—just to have a little fun with him. Then he let him out, and sent him about his business."

"And how long did the madmen stay in power?"

"Oh, a very long time—just how long, I can't say—but weeks. The lunatics had a jolly time of it, you may be sure. They made free with the wine, the food, and the clothing of the true keepers, and lived well, I can tell you."

Here we heard again screams and yells from somewhere in the house. This time, they sounded very near.

"Good heavens!" I cried, "the lunatics must have broken loose."

"I very much fear it is so," said Superintendent Maillard, now very pale.

Loud shouts and oaths were heard beneath the windows and at the door. Plainly, some persons outside were trying to get into the room. The door was being beaten with what seemed to be a sledge hammer.

In the hurry and fear that followed among the diners, I was shocked to see Superintendent Maillard get under the sideboard. I had looked for braver action on his part. At the same time, the man who had wanted to get on the table to make a speech, now jumped up among the bottles and glasses. There he settled himself and began to make a speech which might have been a good one, if it could have been

heard. At the same time, the man, who thought he was a top, set himself to spinning around the room with great force, his arms spread straight out so that he knocked down everybody who got in his way. And now, too, I heard again that popping and fizzing, coming from the one who took himself for a bottle of champagne. The frog-man was croaking away with all his might, and over all arose the loud braying of a donkey. Madame Joyeuse stood up in a corner by the fireplace and kept crying out at the top of her voice, "Cock-a-doodle-de-do-o-o-o-o-!"

161

Except to whoop and yell, no one did anything to hold back the persons breaking in the door. To my horror I saw rush in among the fighting, stamping, scratching, howling mob, about a dozen *things* that looked like a number of big black baboons from Africa. I got a terrible beating—after which I rolled under a sofa and lay still.

Lying there some fifteen minutes, I heard enough to understand what had been going on in that house. Maillard, in telling of the lunatic who led his fellows to rebel against the keepers, was merely relating his own act. He had indeed once been superintendent of the place, some two or three years ago. But he had gone crazy himself, and so became a patient, a fact not known to my traveling companion, who had brought me there. The ten keepers, having been suddenly overpowered, were first well tarred, then carefully feathered, and then shut up in underground cells. They had been there for more than a month, during which time Maillard had used on them his "system" of tar and feathers, with a little bread, and plenty of water. The water was pumped on them daily. At last, one was able to creep out through a sewer, the very evening I was there, and set free all the rest.

I have only to add that, although I have searched every library in Europe for the writings of Doctor *Tarr* and Professor *Fether*, I have not yet found a single book of theirs.

The Spectacles

Many years ago it was the fashion to laugh at the idea of "love at first sight." But those who think and feel deeply have always believed in it. The story I am about to tell will add one more to the many stories that go to prove that there is such a thing as "love at first sight."

I am still a very young man—only twenty-two years of age. My name at this time is a very common one—Simpson. I say "at this time" because it is only within the last year that I have been known as Simpson. I took the name because a distant cousin had left me his fortune, which I could claim only if I took his family name of Simpson. However, I was able to keep my first name, which is Napoleon Bonaparte.

I was sorry to give up my old surname, which was Froissart. My father had been a Monsieur[1] Froissart of Paris. My mother, whom he married when she was fifteen, was the eldest daughter of Croissart the banker. *Her* mother—or my grandmother—was only sixteen when she married. She was the eldest daughter of one Victor Voissart. Strange to say, this Victor Voissart had married a lady with a like-sounding name, a Mademoiselle[2] Moissart. She too was quite a child when she married. And *her* mother was only fourteen when led to the altar. Early marriages are usual in France.

Here, then, are the like-sounding names of Moissart, Voissart, Croissart, and Froissart, all in the direct line of my parents.

As to my looks, I believe I am well made, and have what

[1] French for "Mister."

[2] French for "Miss."

most people would call a handsome face. I am five feet eleven inches tall. My eyes are large and gray. My hair is black and curling. My nose is good enough. But I have one weakness. My eyesight is very weak. I have tried every way to remedy this weakness—short of wearing spectacles. Being young and good-looking, naturally I do not like to wear spectacles, and I would not do so. I know of nothing which so spoils the looks of a young person as spectacles. An eyeglass,[3] on the other hand, gives one an air of smartness and fashion. But I managed to get along without either an eyeglass or spectacles.

One night last winter, I entered a box at the opera, with my friend Talbot. The house was crowded, but we were in time to get front seats which we had ordered earlier. For two hours, Talbot, who is a fanatic about music, had eyes and ears only for the stage. Meantime I amused myself by looking at the people of fashion, in the boxes.

Suddenly my look fell upon a woman with the most beautiful figure I had ever seen. Her face was turned so far toward the stage that I could not, at first, see it well. But the magic of the lovely form! She was sitting, but I judged her to be somewhat above medium height, her form being well-rounded, almost majestic. Her head was partly covered by a cap well suited to add to her charm. Her right arm, draped in the lace of the long loose sleeve now in fashion, rested gracefully on the edge of the box. On her hand sparkled diamonds of great beauty. Her round wrist was set off by a bracelet also richly jeweled. Without doubt, she was a lady of great wealth and fashion.

For some time I sat gazing at her, as if I had been turned to stone. I was feeling the full force of all that has been said and sung about "love at first sight." I knew that I was deeply, madly, forever in love—and this even before I had a full view of her face!

[3] A monocle.

After a time, she chanced to turn her head partly toward me, so that I saw the entire profile of the face. She was even more beautiful than I had expected—and yet there was something about her face that troubled me. I am not able to say just what it was. But the effect was merely to calm and steady the force of my love. Her face had a womanly air. But this was not what moved me. There was something else— something about the face that troubled me, while it added to my keen delight in her beauty. With her were a gentleman, and a very beautiful woman a few years younger than herself.

I was in a state of mind which leads a hasty young man to some rash act. I tried to think of some plan to meet her—or, for the moment, to have a better view of her loveliness. I would have changed my seat for one nearer hers, but the place was crowded, and there was no chance for that.

"Talbot," I said, "*you* have an opera glass. Let me have it."

The Spectacles

"An opera glass! No. What do you think I would be doing with an opera glass?" And he turned hastily back toward the stage.

"But, Talbot," I said, pulling him by the shoulder, "listen to me, will you? Do you see that stage box?—there! No, the next—did you ever see so lovely a woman?"

"She is very beautiful, no doubt," he said.

"I wonder who she can be!"

"Why, don't you know who she is? She is the famous Madame Lalande—the great beauty of the day, the talk of the whole town. Very wealthy, too—a widow, and a great catch—has just come from Paris."

"Do you know her?"

"Yes, I have the honor. In fact, I am an old friend of hers."

"Will you introduce me?"

"Of course, with the greatest of pleasure. When shall it be?"

"At once. I will call upon you tomorrow at one o'clock."

"Very good. And now *do* hold your tongue, *if* you can."

I had to hold my tongue, for Talbot turned back toward the stage, and was deaf to all other talk for the rest of the evening.

In the meantime I kept my gaze on Madame Lalande, and at last was able to get a full front view of her face. It was lovely—this, of course, my heart had told me, before Talbot had said so. Still that strange something about her loveliness kept troubling me. It was, I decided at last, a certain air of gravity, sadness, or still more, weariness. But this, which took from the youth and freshness of her face, gave tenderness and majesty instead. And because of this, she would be ten times more beautiful, to one of my nature.

At last I saw that the lady had noticed my gaze. She turned aside her face, but after some minutes, as if to see if I was still looking, she turned around and again met my burning gaze, for I could not look away. Her large dark eyes lowered, and a deep blush rose to her cheek. But what was my surprise to see that she did not turn her head away, but lifted a double eyeglass and through it, looked at me long and thoughtfully.

Had a thunder bolt fallen at my feet, I could not have been more surprised—surprised, but not offended in the least, for she had acted so naturally, so quietly, with such an air of high breeding. But her act was seen and noticed by others. There was a movement, or buzz, among the crowd. This caused no change in the face and manner of Madame Lalande. Having finished her study of me—if such it was— she dropped the glass and turned her face quietly to the stage.

Her profile now being turned toward me, I gazed at her as before, though I knew my act was rude. Soon I saw her head slowly and slightly change its position. I began to believe that the lady, while sitting as if looking at the stage, was in fact watching me. It is useless to say what effect such an act, on the part of so charming a person, had upon me.

Having thus watched me for some minutes, she spoke to the gentleman who was with her, and I understood by the glances of both, that she spoke of me. Then Madame Lalande turned again toward the stage. But after a short time I saw her unfold the eyeglass, and the second time she looked me over from head to foot. There was again a buzz from the crowd, but she kept the same heedless calm.

Her interest in me threw me into a perfect fever of love. I forgot everything but the majesty and beauty of the woman before my eyes, and when at last she looked toward me again, I made a slight bow. She blushed deeply—turned away her eyes—and slowly, as if with caution, looked around to see whether my rash act had been noticed. Then she leaned over toward the gentleman who sat by her side. I felt a burning sense of having been rude, and a vision of pistols, on the morrow, flashed through my brain. But the lady merely handed the gentleman a program, without speaking.

The Spectacles

The next moment, she turned her bright eyes fully upon me, and with a smile that showed a bright line of pearly teeth, she nodded twice.

I will not dwell upon my joy. But if ever a man was mad with happiness, it was myself at that moment. I loved. This was my *first* love—so I felt it to be. It was "love at first sight"—and at "first sight" too it had been *returned!* Yes, returned. How and why should I doubt it for a moment? What else would have moved her to act so—a lady so beautiful—so wealthy—of so lofty a place in society? Yes, she loved me—as suddenly , as blindly, as I loved her.

The curtain fell, the crowd rose, and the usual slow movement toward the doors began. I tried to force my way nearer Madame Lalande, but failed. At last, I gave up the chase, and started homeward, happy because Talbot had promised to introduce me, in due form upon the morrow.

This morrow at last came. That is to say, a day finally dawned upon a weary night of longing. Then the hours until one dragged along. But everything comes to an end, and finally the hour came. At one o'clock sharp I was at Talbot's door.

"Out," said the footman.

"Out!" I said, staggering back. "Let me tell you, my fine fellow, Mr. Talbot is *not* out. What do you mean?"

"Nothing, sir; only Mr. Talbot is not in. That's all. He left right after breakfast, and said he would not be in town again for a week."

I stood like one turned to stone by horror and rage. I tried to reply, but my tongue would not move. I turned away, pale with rage, inwardly cursing the whole tribe of Talbots. It was plain he had quite forgotten his word to me— had forgotten it as soon as it was spoken. He was never very careful about keeping a promise.

There was nothing else I could do. I strolled up the street, asking every friend that I met about Madame Lalande. All knew of her—many knew her only by sight—but she had been in town only a few weeks, and few knew her well enough to take the liberty of making a call to introduce me. As I stood speaking of her to a friend, he cried out: "As I live, there she is!"

I looked, and saw her in an open carriage, passing slowly down the street. With her was the same younger lady who had sat in her box at the opera.

"Her companion also wears very well," said my friend. "A lively air and some powder will do wonders. Upon my word, she looks better than she did at Paris, five years ago. A beautiful woman still—don't you think so, Froissart?— Simpson, I mean."

"*Still* beautiful!" I cried. "And why shouldn't she be! She is lovely as a star."

"Ha! ha! ha! Simpson, you have great tact."

As the carriage of Madame Lalande rolled by us, she saw and knew me, and openly gave me a smile.

The Spectacles

As for an introduction, I had to give up hope of that until Talbot came back. In the meantime, I went about all the time, hoping to see her. After two weeks, I saw her again at the theater. Every day during this time I had asked for Talbot at his place, and every day had been thrown into a fit of wrath by the everlasting "not come home yet" of his footman.

Madame Lalande, I learned, lived in Paris. She might suddenly return there—return before Talbot came back. The thought was too terrible to bear. I must act at once. In a word, I followed her home from the theater, and thus learned her address. The next morning I sent her a long letter, in which I poured out my whole heart, and ended with an offer of my hand.

In an agony I waited for the reply. After what seemed a century, it came. Yes, *it came.* I really had a letter from the beautiful Madame Lalande! She had *not* scorned me! She had *not* sheltered herself in silence! She had *not* returned my letter unopened! She had written me a letter with her own lovely fingers. It ran thus:

> Monsieur Simpson vill pardonne me for not write de butefull tong of his countree so vell as might. It is only late dat I come and not yet ave de time for it to study.
>
> I vill now say dat—alas!—you ave guess but too true. Need I say more? Alas! am I not already speak too mosch?
>
> Eugénie Lalande

I kissed the note a million times, and no doubt gave way to my great joy in a thousand other ways, which I do not now remember.

Still Talbot *would not* return. I wrote to him. He replied. He was held by business—but would soon return. I wrote again, begging him, if he could not return at once, to send me a letter of introduction. I wrote again to beg him to hurry the letter. My letters were returned by *that* footman, who had joined his master in the country. The fellow had written the following in pencil:

The master left here yesterday, for parts unknown—did not say when he would be back—so thought best to return letters, knowing your handwriting, and how you is always, more or less, in a hurry.

Stubbs

It would do no good to be angry. And I had one thing to fall back on—my native boldness in society—my cheek, if you like to call it so. Since her letter to me, I had been in the habit of watching her house. I had learned that she went, about dusk, for a walk in the public square before her place. With her went only a servant. Here, in the gray of a sweet summer evening, I met her on the path. To manage the servant, I greeted her with the air of a person well known to her. She took the cue at once, and held out her hand. The servant fell behind. And now, with heart full to overflowing, we spoke of our love.

I begged her to marry me at once, tomorrow. She said that we must not shock society by such a sudden move. She told me to remember that I really did not know who she was. She begged me—with a sigh—to think the matter over—to be sure that I really loved her. She spoke these words as the shadows of sweet twilight gathered darker and darker around us. And then, with a gentle touch of her fairylike fingers, she overthrew in a single sweet moment, all that she had said against my so eager love.

I replied as only a true lover can, and at last she held out against me no longer. But, there was yet something else, she said, that I must know. It was a trying thing for a woman to speak of, but still, for *me*, she would do so. It was about her age that she would speak. Did I know that she was older than

The Spectacles

I? The husband should be at least a few years—perhaps even fifteen or twenty—older than the wife. She herself had always believed that it was unnatural for a wife to be older than the husband, and likely—alas!—to result in unhappiness. She knew, she said, that I was not more than twenty-two, but I did not know that she was several years older than that.

"My sweet Eugénie," I cried, "what are you talking about? You are a few years older than I. But what of it? I am twenty-two, you say. Granted. Indeed, you may as well call me, at once, twenty-three. Now, you cannot be older than—older than—than—than—"

She did not break in to finish my sentence, for she was bending forward to pick up something she had dropped on the grass. I at once picked it up and handed it to her. It was a locket.

"Keep it!" she said, with one of her sweetest smiles. "It is my picture. On the back of it you will find an inscription giving my age when the locket was made. You can look at it in the morning. Now you may take me home."

The mansion was a fine one and, I believe, furnished in good taste. But it was dark when we went in, and as in many American mansions of the better sort, in the heat of summer, lamps were not lighted during that most pleasant time, early evening. About an hour after I came in, a single shaded lamp was lit in the principal drawing-room, and this room—I could see from where we sat—was arranged with unusually good taste, even splendor.

It was, without doubt, the happiest evening of my life. She sat beside me and we talked, long and earnestly. She made me tell of my earlier life, and listened with breathless interest. I remembered that she had been frank to tell me about her age, and I felt that I had no right to keep back anything from her. I told her not only all my little vices, but spoke also of my more serious failings—my wild college days—my debts—my weak eyes.

"If you had not told me you have weak eyes," said

Madame Lalande laughing, "I should hardly have known of it. By the way, do you remember this?"

As she spoke, she twirled in her fingers the double eyeglass which she had turned upon me at the opera.

"Do I remember it!" I cried, pressing the little hand that held the glasses. "Of course I remember it!"

"Oh, well, my beloved," she said with a certain serious manner that rather puzzled me, "you have asked me to marry you tomorrow. If I give my promise, will you do me a little favor in return?"

"Name it!" I cried. "But it is done before you name it!"

"Then, for my sake you will overcome a little weakness, which if you do not correct, will surely bring you into a scrape, sooner or later. What I would say is that I wish you to wear spectacles—now, now—hush!—remember you have already promised to wear them, before I asked you. *For my sake*, you shall take this little toy which I hold in my hand. By a small turn thus—or thus—it can be fitted to the eyes in the form of spectacles, or worn in the waistcoat pocket as an eyeglass. But you have already promised to wear it as spectacles, *for my sake*."

This business—I must say—bothered me not a little. But I gave my promise with as much warmth as I could muster at the moment.

"It shall be done!" I said. "Tonight, I wear this dear eyeglass in my pocket, over my heart. But tomorrow—the day that I call you wife—I will wear it upon my nose—and there wear it ever after."

We now spoke of plans for the morrow. Talbot, she told me, had just come back to town. I was to see him at once, and come for her early in the morning. We would then go to the house of a priest and be married, then drop off Talbot, and start forth on a short tour of the East, leaving society to say what it pleased.

Having planned all this, I took leave at once, and went in search of Talbot. But I could not wait until tomorrow to look at the locket. On the way, I stepped into a hotel and looked at the picture, by the aid of a powerful glass. The face was very beautiful—the same large eyes—the same proud nose—those dark curls—all the same. I turned the picture over, and saw the words: "Eugénie Lalande, aged 27 years and 7 months."

I found Talbot was at home, and at once told him of my good fortune. He was surprised, of course, but gave me his good wishes, and offered to help in any way he could.

In a word, we carried out our plan to the letter. Ten minutes after the wedding, I was in a close carriage with Madame Lalande—with Mrs. Simpson, I should say—and driving at a great rate out of the city. We had planned to make the first stop at C——, a village about twenty miles away. There we could get an early breakfast and some rest before going farther on our journey.

At four o'clock, then, the carriage drew up at the door of the inn in C——. I handed my dear wife out, and ordered breakfast. Meanwhile, we were shown into a small parlor, and sat down to wait. It was now nearly daylight, and as I gazed at my angel wife, the idea came all at once into my head, that this was really the first time I had enjoyed a near sight of her lovely face by daylight.

"And now, my love," said she, taking my hand, "you have not forgotten that you gave me a promise, you know, to wear the spectacles."

Mrs. Simpson folded her arms and sat bolt upright in her chair, in a somewhat stiff and prim manner.

"My beautiful Eugénie, I will keep my promise. See! Behold! They are becoming—rather—are they not?" And here, having arranged the glasses in the form of spectacles, I set them upon my nose.

"Good gracious me!" I cried, almost at the very moment the glasses settled upon my nose, "why, what *can* be the matter with these glasses?"

Taking them quickly off, I wiped them carefully, and put

them on again. Why, what in the name of everything hideous, did this mean? Could I believe my eyes?—*could* I? Was that—was that *rouge*? And were those—were those *wrinkles* upon the face of Eugénie Lalande? And oh, Jupiter, and all the gods and goddesses, little and big—what—what—*what* had become of her teeth?

I dashed the spectacles to the floor, leaped to my feet, and stood over Mrs. Simpson, speechless with terror and rage.

"Well," said she, "what now? If you don't like me, you shouldn't buy a pig in a poke."

"You wretch!" said I, catching my breath, "you—you— you old hag!"

"Old? Not so very old, after all. Not a single day more than eighty-two."

"Eighty-two!" I cried, staggering to the wall. "Eighty-two hundred thousand baboons! The picture said twenty-seven years and seven months!"

"To be sure! That is so. Very true. But then the picture has been made these fifty-five years. When I married my second husband, Monsieur Lalande, I had the picture made for my daughter by my first husband, Monsieur Moissart."

"Moissart!" said I.

"Yes, Moissart. What do *you* know about Moissart?"

"Nothing, you old fright! I know nothing about him at all—only I had a great-grandmother named Moissart."

"It is a good name. And so is Voissart—that is a very good name, too. My daughter, Mademoiselle Moissart, married Monsieur Voissart. Both good names."

"Moissart and Voissart!" I cried. "What do you mean?"

"What do I mean? I mean Moissart and Voissart. My daughter's daughter, Mademoiselle Voissart, married Monsieur Croissart. And then again, my daughter's grand-daughter, Mademoisselle Croissart, married Monsieur Froissart."

"Froissart!" I said, beginning to feel faint.

"Yes," she said, leaning back in her chair, and stretching out her lower limbs at great length. "But Monsieur Froissart was a fool—a great big dunce like yourself—for he left beautiful France to come to this stupid America. And when he got here, he went and had a *very* stupid, a *very, very* stupid son, so I hear. His name is Napoleon Bonaparte Froissart. But I have not had the pleasure to meet him—neither I nor my companion Madame Stéphanie Lalande."

Here she snatched the cap from her head, and with it a wig of the most beautiful black hair. I sank weakly into a chair.

"Why, you old serpent," I cried, "Napoleon Bonaparte Froissart—that is *me*—that's *me*—don't you hear? that's *me*." Here I screamed at the top of my voice, "*I* am Napoleon Bonaparte Froissart! And if I haven't married my great-great-grandmother, I wish I may die this minute!"

The Spectacles

In sober fact, Madame Eugénie Lalande—now Simpson—formerly Moissart—was indeed my great-great-grandmother. In her youth, she had been beautiful. At eighty-two, she still had the majestic form and the large eyes of her girlhood. By the aid of these, with powder, rouge, false hair, false teeth, and the dressmakers, she was able to hold a footing among the aging beauties of Paris. She was very wealthy, and being left a widow the second time, without children, she had thought of me in America, to whom she could leave her fortune. She had come to the United States, bringing with her a Madame Stéphanie Lalande, a lovely distant cousin of her last husband.

At the opera, my great-great-grandomther had noticed me, and looking through her eyeglass was struck by the family look that she saw in me. Knowing that I was in the city, she asked the gentleman with her if I could be Napoleon Bonaparte Froissart. He told her that I was, and she looked at me again. When I bowed, she returned my greeting, thinking that by some odd chance, I had learned who she was. When I asked Talbot who she was, he thought, of course, that I was asking about the younger Madame Lalande, and had truthfully answered that she was a "great beauty."

My great-great-grandmother had met Talbot the next day, and naturally their talk turned to me. She learned of my weak eyesight—for this weakness was known to all, though I did not dream it was so noticeable. In a word, my good old great-great-grandmother then understood that I had not known who she was, but had been making a fool of myself by courting a strange old woman in public. To punish me, she made a plot, with Talbot to aid her. He left town to keep out of my way. All my questions to others about the "lovely widow, Madame Lalande" had been taken to refer to the younger Madame Stéphanie Lalande.

The priest who had pretended to marry us, was no priest, but a good friend of Talbot's. Therefore, luckily, I am *not* married to my great-great-grandmother. But I *am* the hus-

The Spectacles

band of Madame Stéphanie Lalande, for my good old great-great-grandmother troubled herself to make a match between us. The old lady now lives with us, and will leave all her wealth to me when she dies—if she ever does.

Needless to say, the glasses that she gave me were not her own, but a pair made for me. In fact, they fit me to a T. I wear my spectacles all the time now.

POEMS

The Raven
The Bells
Annabel Lee
El Dorado
Sonnet to Science
To Helen

The Raven

like that line.

Once upon a midnight dreary, while I pondered, weak and
    weary,
Over many a quaint and curious volume of forgotten lore—
While I nodded, nearly napping, suddenly there came a
    tapping,
As of some one gently rapping, rapping at my chamber door.
" 'Tis some visitor," I muttered, "tapping at my chamber
    door—
    Only this and nothing more."

Ah, distinctly I remember it was in the bleak December;
And each separate dying ember wrought its ghost upon the
    floor.
Eagerly I wished the morrow—vainly I had sought to borrow
From my books surcease[1] of sorrow—sorrow for the lost
    Lenore—
For the rare and radiant maiden whom the angels name
    Lenore—
    Nameless *here* for evermore.

And the silken, sad, uncertain rustling of each purple curtain
Thrilled me—filled me with fantastic terrors never felt before;
So that now, to still the beating of my heart, I stood re-
    peating,
" 'Tis some visitor entreating entrance at my chamber door—

[1] The end.

The Raven

Some late visitor entreating entrance at my chamber door—
    This it is and nothing more."

Presently my soul grew stronger; hesitating then no longer,
"Sir," said I, "or Madam, truly your forgiveness I implore;
But the fact is I was napping, and so gently you came rap-
        ping,
And so faintly you came tapping, tapping at my chamber
        door,
That I scarce was sure I heard you"—here I opened wide
        the door—
    Darkness there and nothing more.

Deep into the darkness peering, long I stood there wondering,
        fearing,
Doubting, dreaming dreams no mortal ever dared to dream
        before;
But the silence was unbroken, and the stillness gave no token,
And the only word there spoken was the whispered word,
        "Lenore?"
This I whispered, and an echo murmured back the word
        "Lenore!"—
    Merely this, and nothing more.

Back into the chamber turning, all my soul within me burn-
        ing,
Soon again I heard a tapping somewhat louder than before.
"Surely," said I, "surely that is something at my window
        lattice;
Let me see, then, what thereat is, and this mystery explore—
Let my heart be still a moment and this mystery explore—
    'Tis the wind and nothing more!"

Open here I flung the shutter, when, with many a flirt and
        flutter,
In there stepped a stately Raven of the saintly days of yore;

my
stanza

182

Not the least obeisance[2] made he, not a minute stopped or
    stayed he;
But with mien[3] of lord or lady, perched above my chamber
    door—
Perched upon a bust of Pallas[4] just above my chamber door—
    Perched, and sat, and nothing more.

Then this ebony bird beguiling[5] my sad fancy into smiling,
By the grave and stern decorum[6] of the countenance it
    wore,
"Though thy crest be shorn and shaven, thou," I said, "art
    sure no craven,
Ghastly grim and ancient Raven wandering from the Nightly
    shore—
Tell me what thy lordly name is on the Night's Plutonian[7]
    shore!—
    Quoth the Raven, "Nevermore."

Much I marveled this ungainly fowl to hear discourse[8] so
    plainly,
Though its answer little meaning—little relevancy[9] bore;
For we cannot help agreeing that no living human being
Ever yet was blessed with seeing bird above his chamber
    door—
Bird or beast upon the sculptured bust above his chamber
    door,
    With such name as "Nevermore."

[2] Bow.
[3] Manner.
[4] Greek goddess of wisdom, Pallas Athena.
[5] Charming or diverting.
[6] Dignity.
[7] Referring to Pluto, Roman god of the underworld.
[8] To speak.
[9] Fitness or suitability.

The Raven

But the Raven, sitting lonely on that placid bust, spoke only
That one word, as if his soul in that one word he did out-
      pour.
Nothing further then he uttered—not a feather then he
      fluttered—
Till I scarcely more than muttered—"Other friends have
      flown before:
On the morrow *he* will leave me, as my Hopes have flown
      before."
      Then the bird said, "Nevermore."

Startled at the stillness broken by reply so aptly spoken,
"Doubtless," said I, "what it utters is its only stock and
      store,
Caught from some unhappy master whom unmerciful Disas-
      ter
Followed fast and followed faster till his songs one burden[10]
      bore—
Till the dirges[11] of his Hope that melancholy burden bore
Of 'Never—nevermore'."

But the Raven still beguiling all my fancy into smiling,
Straight I wheeled a cushioned seat in front of bird, and
      bust and door;
Then upon the velvet sinking, I betook myself to linking
Fancy unto fancy, thinking what this ominous[12] bird of
      yore—
What this grim, ungainly, ghastly, gaunt, and ominous bird
      of yore
      Meant in croaking "Nevermore."

This I sat engaged in guessing, but no syllable expressing
To the fowl whose fiery eyes now burned into my bosom's
      core;

[10] Theme or main idea.
[11] Songs of grief.
[12] Foreshadowing evil.

This and more I sat divining,[13] with my head at ease reclining
On the cushion's velvet lining that the lamplight gloated
o'er,
But whose velvet violet lining with the lamplight gloating
o'er,
She shall press, ah, nevermore!

Then, methought, the air grew denser, perfumed from an
unseen censer[14]
Swung by seraphim[15] whose foot-falls tinkled on the tufted
floor.
"Wretch,"[16] I cried, "thy God hath lent thee—by these
angels he hath sent thee
Respite—respite and nepenthe,[17] from thy memories of
Lenore;
Quaff, oh, quaff this kind nepenthe and forget this lost
Lenore!"
Quoth the Raven, "Nevermore."

"Prophet!" said I, "thing of evil!—prophet still, if bird or
devil!—
Whether Tempter sent, or whether tempest tossed thee here
ashore,
Desolate yet all undaunted, on this desert land enchanted—
On this home by Horror haunted—tell me truly, I implore—
Is there—*is* there balm in Gilead?[18]—tell me—tell me, I
implore!"
Quoth the Raven, "Nevermore."

[13] Guessing, wondering.

[14] A container for perfumes or incense.

[15] Plural of *seraph*, an angel.

[16] The poet here addresses himself.

[17] A drug to drown pain or sorrow.

[18] A phrase from the Bible. Gilead is a mountain district in Palestine. Balm of Gilead is a tree gum valued for its sweet odor and its medical uses. As used in the Bible and here, the phrase means "relief from pain or grief."

"Prophet!" said I, "thing of evil!—prophet still, if bird or
    devil!
By that Heaven that bends above us—by that God we both
    adore—
Tell this soul with sorrow laden if, within the distant
    Aidenn,[19]
It shall clasp a sainted maiden whom the angels name Len-
    ore—
Clasp a rare and radiant maiden whom the angels name
    Lenore."
    Quoth the Raven, "Nevermore."

[19] Eden.

186

The Raven

"Be that word our sign of parting, bird or fiend!" I shrieked,
     upstarting—
"Get thee back into the tempest and the Night's Plutonian
     shore!
Leave no black plume as a token of that lie thy soul hath
     spoken!
Leave my loneliness unbroken!—quit the bust above my
     door!
Take thy beak from out my heart, and take thy form from
     off my door!"
     Quoth the Raven, "Nevermore."

And the Raven, never flitting, still is sitting, *still* is sitting
On the pallid[20] bust of Pallas just above my chamber door;
And his eyes have all the seeming of a demon's that is dream-
     ing,
And the lamplight o'er him streaming throws his shadow on
     the floor;
And my soul from out that shadow that lies floating on
     the floor
     Shall be lifted—nevermore!

that was a pretty great poem!

[20] Pale, made of marble.

The Bells

Hear the sledges with the bells—
      Silver bells!
What a world of merriment their melody foretells!
   How they tinkle, tinkle, tinkle
     In the icy air of night!
  While the stars that oversprinkle
  All the heavens, seem to twinkle
   With a crystalline delight;
  Keeping time, time, time,
  In a sort of runic[1] rhyme,
To the tintinnabulation[2] that so musically wells
  From the bells, bells, bells, bells,
      Bells, bells, bells—
From the jingling and the tinkling of the bells.

II

  Hear the mellow wedding bells,
      Golden bells!
What a world of happiness their harmony foretells!
   Through the balmy air of night
   How they ring out their delight!
    From the molten-golden notes,
      And all in tune,
    What a liquid ditty floats
  To the turtledove that listens while she gloats
     On the moon!

[1] Secret or mysterious.
[2] The sound of bells.

Oh, from out the sounding cells,
What a gush of euphony[3] voluminously[4] wells!
How it swells!
How it dwells
On the Future! how it tells
Of the rapture that impels
To the swinging and the ringing
Of the bells, bells, bells,
Of the bells, bells, bells, bells,
Bells, bells, bells—
To the rhyming and the chiming of the bells!

[3] Pleasing or sweet sound.
[4] Large, swelling.

The Bells

III

Hear the loud alarum bells—
  Brazen bells!
What a tale of terror, now, their turbulency[5] tells!
 In the startled ear of night
 How they scream out their affright!
  Too much horrified to speak,
  They can only shriek, shriek,
   Out of tune,
In a clamorous appealing to the mercy of the fire,
In a mad expostulation[6] with the deaf and frantic fire,
  Leaping higher, higher, higher,
  With a desperate desire
   And a resolute endeavor
   Now—now to sit or never
  By the side of the pale-faced moon.
   Oh, the bells, bells, bells!
   What a tale their terror tells
    Of Despair!
  How they clang, and clash, and roar!
  What a horror they outpour
On the bosom of the palpitating[7] air!
   Yet the ear, it fully knows,
    By the twanging
    And the clanging,
   How the danger ebbs and flows;
   Yet the ear distinctly tells,
    In the jangling,
    And the wrangling,

[5] Noisy unrest.
[6] Earnest protest.
[7] Fluttering, throbbing.

How the danger sinks and swells,
By the sinking or the swelling in the anger of the bells—
    Of the bells—
  Of the bells, bells, bells, bells,
     Bells, bells, bells—
In the clamor and the clangor of the bells!

IV

Hear the tolling of the bells—
    Iron bells!
What a world of solemn thought their monody[8]
                 compels!
  In the silence of the night,
  How we shiver with affright
At the melancholy menace of their tone!
  For every sound that floats
  From the rust within their throats
    Is a groan.
And the people—ah, the people—
They that dwell up in the steeple,
    All alone,
And who tolling, tolling, tolling,
  In that muffled monotone,
Feel a glory in so rolling
  On the human heart a stone—
They are neither man nor woman—
They are neither brute nor human—
    They are Ghouls:[9]
  And their king it is who tolls,
  And he rolls, rolls, rolls,
    Rolls

[8] A poem in which a death is lamented.
[9] Evil spirits who, according to legend, rob graves, and feed on corpses.

The Bells

A paean[10] from the bells!
And his merry bosom swells
  With the paean of the bells!
And he dances, and he yells;
Keeping time, time, time,
In a sort of runic rhyme
    To the paean of the bells—
      Of the bells:
Keeping time, time, time,
In a sort of runic rhyme,
    To the throbbing of the bells—
Of the bells, bells, bells—
    To the sobbing of the bells—
Keeping time, time, time,
    As he knells,[11] knells, knells,
In a happy runic rhyme,
    To the rolling of the bells—
Of the bells, bells, bells—
    To the tolling of the bells—
Of the bells, bells, bells, bells,
      Bells, bells, bells—
To the moaning and the groaning of the bells.

[10] A song of praise or joy.
[11] Tolls.

Annabel Lee

It was many and many a year ago,
    In a kingdom by the sea,
That a maiden there lived whom you may know
    By the name of Annabel Lee;
And this maiden she lived with no other thought
    Than to love and be loved by me.

I was a child and she was a child,
    In this kingdom by the sea,
But we loved with a love that was more than love—
    I and my Annabel Lee—
With a love that the winged seraphs of heaven
    Coveted[1] her and me.

And this was the reason that, long ago,
    In this kingdom by the sea,
A wind blew out of a cloud, chilling
    My beautiful Annabel Lee;
So that her highborn kinsmen came
    And bore her away from me,
To shut her up in a sepulcher[2]
    In this kingdom by the sea.

The angels, not half so happy in Heaven,
    Went envying her and me—
Yes!—that was the reason (as all men know,
    In this kingdom by the sea)
That the wind came out of the cloud, by night,
    Chilling and killing my Annabel Lee.

[1] Envied.
[2] Tomb.

Annabel Lee

But our love it was stonger by far than the love
    Of those who were older than we—
    Of many far wiser than we—
And neither the angels in heaven above,
    Nor the demons down under the sea,
Can ever dissever my soul from the soul
    Of the beautiful Annabel Lee.

For the moon never beams without bringing me dreams
    Of the beautiful Annabel Lee;
And the stars never rise but I feel the bright eyes
    Of the beautiful Annabel Lee;
And so, all the night tide, I lie down by the side
Of my darling—my darling—my life and my bride,
    In her sepulcher there by the sea—
    In her tomb by the sounding sea.

194

El Dorado

Gayly bedight,[1]
A gallant knight,
In sunshine and in shadow,
Had journeyed long,
Singing a song,
In search of El Dorado.[2]

But he grew old—
This knight so bold—
And o'er his heart a shadow
Fell as he found
No spot of ground
That looked like El Dorado.

And, as his strength
Failed him at length,
He met a pilgrim shadow—[3]
"Shadow," said he,
"Where can it be—
This land of El Dorado?"

"Over the Mountains
Of the Moon,
Down the Valley of the Shadow,
Ride, boldly ride,"
The shade[3] replied—
"If you seek for El Dorado!"

[1] Decked out, arrayed.
[2] A legendary city of South America, sought by early Spanish explorers for its gold; any place of fabulous riches. In this poem, the word is used as a symbol of an ideal, wish, or dream that can never be gained.
[3] Spirit or ghost.

Sonnet to Science

Science! true daughter of Old Time thou art!
  Who alterest all things with thy peering eyes.
Why preyest thou thus upon the poet's heart,
  Vulture,[1] whose wings are dull realities?

How should he love thee? or how deem thee wise,
  Who wouldst not leave him in his wandering
To seek for treasure in the jeweled skies,
  Albeit[2] he soared with an undaunted wing?

Hast thou not dragged Diana[3] from her car?
  And driven the Hamadryad[3] from the wood
To seek a shelter in some happier star?
  Hast thou not torn the Naiad[3] from her flood,

The Elfin[4] from the green grass, and from me
The summer dream beneath the tamarind tree?

[1] This word is applied to Science.

[2] Although.

[3] According to ancient Greek myths, the moon was the maiden Diana, who nightly drove her chariot across the sky; a spirit or wood nymph, called a dryad or hamadryad, lived in every tree; and water nymphs, called naiads, lived in lakes and streams.

[4] An elf.

To Helen

Helen, thy beauty is to me
  Like those Nicaean barks[1] of yore,
That gently, o'er a perfumed sea,
  The weary, wayworn wanderer bore
  To his own native shore.

On desperate seas long wont to roam,
  Thy hyacinth hair, thy classic face,
Thy Naiad airs have brought me home
  To the glory that was Greece
And the grandeur that was Rome.

[1] A boat used by the people of the ancient city of Nicaea.

To Helen

> Lo! in yon brilliant window-niche
> How statue-like I see thee stand,
> The agate lamp within thy hand!
> Ah, Psyche,[2] from the regions which
> Are Holy Land!

[2] The human soul or spirit. The beauty of this poem lies in the mere *suggestion* of a meaning; certain words can not be given a *definite* meaning.

Reviewing Your Reading

The Gold Bug

Finding the Main Idea

1. Another good title for this story might be
   (A) "Jupiter's Fear" (B) "The Left Eye of the Skull"
   (C) "Two Skeletons" (D) "The Strange Madness of
   William Legrand"

Remembering Detail

2. When Jupiter climbs out along the branch of the tree,
   he finds a
   (A) gold bug (B) skull (C) treasure (D) dead bird
3. The men guess the treasure to be worth
   (A) very little (B) fifty thousand dollars (C) a million
   and a half dollars (D) five million dollars
4. What pun helps Legrand solve the code?
   (A) The picture of the *kid* and Captain *Kidd* (B) The
   rhyme of *goat* and *boat* (C) The *gold* bug and the *gold*
   of the treasure (D) The rhyme of *Legrand* and *hand*
5. The code phrase "bishop's hostel" refers to
   (A) an old hotel (B) a church (C) a large rock (D) a
   50-room castle

Drawing Conclusions

6. The narrator begins to dig eagerly the second time because Legrand
   (A) would kill him if he didn't (B) seems sure and determined (C) is tired of doing all the work (D) has
   sent Jupiter away

Using Your Reason

7. Legrand's mind works most like the mind of a
   (A) sailor (B) murderer (C) pirate (D) detective

8. An illogical part of the story is that
   (A) the dog jumps into the narrator's lap at the beginning of the story (B) Legrand sends Jupiter to buy
   the equipment (C) Jupiter finds that a branch of the
   tree is rotten (D) Legrand doesn't tell the narrator
   about the code until after they find the treasure
9. Legrand drops the gold bug instead of a small weight
   through the skull because he
   (A) is angry at his friend (B) had to use gold to find
   gold (C) wants to frighten Jupiter (D) forgot to bring
   a weight
10. When they were digging the first hole, the narrator said
    that although he was puzzled he "began to dig with a
    good will." He would have meant the same thing if he
    had said that he began to dig
    (A) slowly (B) eagerly (C) quickly (D) sadly

Identifying the Mood
11. Which of the following best describes how the narrator
    feels during the first part of the story?
    (A) Greedy (B) Happy (C) Doubtful (D) Angry

Thinking it Over
1. What does Legrand know about the English language
   that helps him solve the code?
2. What other special information does Legrand know (or
   guess) that helps him understand the message?
3. Do you agree with Legrand's ideas on how the skeletons
   wound up in the pit? If you don't, how do you think
   they got there?
4. The name of this story is "The Gold Bug." How important to the story is the gold bug? Is the bug necessary to help the men find the treasure? Why or why
   not? Is the bug a symbol of anything? What does it
   symbolize to Legrand? to Jupiter? to the narrator?
   to you?

The Murders in the Rue Morgue

Finding the Main Idea

1. The author is mostly interested in telling how
(A) a sailor loses his pet orangutan (B) Dupin solves a murder case (C) Madame L'Espanaye gets her money (D) the narrator refuses to believe Dupin's ideas

Remembering Detail

2. Where is the body of Madame L'Espanaye found?
(A) In the chimney (B) On the bed (C) On the floor beneath the table (D) In the yard behind the building
3. Most of the witnesses agree that the gruff voice was that of a
(A) German (B) Russian (C) Frenchman (D) Spaniard
4. Dupin realizes that the second window is fastened by
(A) a nail (B) the window sash (C) a heavy rope (D) a secret spring
5. What does Dupin find at the foot of the lightning rod?
(A) A pistol (B) A piece of ribbon (C) A newspaper (D) A razor

Drawing Conclusions

6. Dupin guesses that the "shrill voice" wasn't human because
(A) none of the witnesses agreed on what language it spoke (B) two witnesses said that it sounded like a monkey's (C) he knows that no human voice can sound "shrill" (D) one witness said it was "harsh," not "shrill"

Using Your Reason

7. Adolphe Le Bon is arrested for the murders probably because

(A) he was the last one known to have visited the two women (B) all the witnesses recognized his voice (C) he knew the women personally (D) one witness saw him sliding down the lightning rod

8. When the narrator says he felt "a creeping of the flesh," he would have meant the same thing if he had said he felt
(A) afraid (B) angry (C) sad (D) happy

Identifying the Mood

9. When the sailor tells the story of the murder, he feels
(A) frightened (B) sorrowful (C) angry (D) happy
10. At the end of the story, the Prefect of Police is
(A) sad (B) jealous (C) fearful (D) humorous

Reading for Deeper Meaning

11. What power of Dupin's is most obvious in this story?
(A) His wealth (B) His courage (C) His ability to reason (D) His great physical strength

Thinking it Over

1. At what point in Dupin's discussion of the case did you become aware that the murderer wasn't human? What made you realize this?

2. Do you agree with all of Dupin's conclusions? For example, Dupin says that there was no motive of robbery, because 4,000 francs were found in the room. But if a human murderer had heard the witnesses at the front door, he or she may have left without the money. Why? Are there any other questionable conclusions by Dupin? If so, what are they?

3. At the end of the story, the sailor is said to receive "a large sum" for the orangutan. Do you think this is fair? Why or why not?

4. What kind of man is Dupin? How would you describe his mind? his character? How does he react when he

views the scene of the murder? Is he horror-stricken? Why do you suppose he isn't? Would you like to be like Dupin? Why or why not?

The Purloined Letter

Finding the Main Idea

1. The main idea of the story is that
(A) it is easy to find a stolen letter (B) an evil person will always get caught (C) only a fool would try to outwit the Prefect of Police (D) a problem may have a very obvious answer

Remembering Detail

2. How does the minister use the stolen letter?
(A) To play a trick on Dupin (B) To get rid of Dupin (C) To place political pressure on the owner of the letter (D) To get money from the owner of the letter
3. In looking for the letter, the police do all of the following EXCEPT
(A) question the minister (B) search the minister (C) examine the minister's house (D) examine the houses next to the minister's
4. The police do not find the letter because
(A) the hiding place is out in the open (B) the minister has it in his shoe (C) the minister has burned it
(D) there really is no letter
5. How much money does Dupin receive for solving the case?
(A) No money (B) Ten thousand francs (C) Twenty-five thousand francs (D) Fifty thousand francs

Drawing Conclusions

6. The dark glasses Dupin wears to the minister's house enable Dupin to

(A) pretend he is blind (B) see through walls and doors
(C) look all around without being noticed (D) keep
the sun out of his eyes

Using Your Reason

7. The mind of the Prefect of Police works most like
   that of a
   (A) poet (B) bricklayer (C) musician (D) gambler
8. Dupin has paid someone to fire a gun in order to
   (A) distract the minister (B) kill the minister
   (C) frighten the Prefect of Police (D) upset the narrator of the story

Identifying the Mood

9. Which of the following best describes the character of
   the minister?
   (A) Nervous and frightened (B) Innocent and friendly
   (C) Cunning and ruthless (D) Noble and courageous

Reading for Deeper Meaning

10. In this story, Dupin's method of working might be
    called
    (A) making the lucky guess (B) heads I win, tails you
    lose (C) thinking like a schoolboy (D) putting your-
    self in the mind of another

Thinking it Over

1. The story, as written, does not make clear how the
   minister can change the appearance of the letter so
   completely. But if you realize that the letter is in an
   envelope, it becomes more obvious. How does the
   minister disguise the letter and the envelope?
2. Dupin explains how, as a boy, he won everyone's
   marbles in a game called "even or odd." What was his
   method of winning? What does this have to do with
   how he finds the stolen letter?

3. When the Prefect of Police says that he has been asked to find the stolen letter, Dupin says, "And a wiser agent I suppose could not be found." With this answer, Dupin is being a little sarcastic. What is sarcasm? What are some other examples of sarcasm in this story?

The Black Cat

Finding the Main Idea
1. The author is mostly interested in telling how
(A) a cat avenges a murder (B) drunkenness can lead to violence (C) people can be cruel to their pets (D) the police solve a difficult case

Remembering Detail
2. Where is the narrator as he tells this story?
(A) In a hospital (B) In his cellar (C) In a prison cell (D) In his parents' house
3. The white spot on the second cat's breast begins to look like
(A) an ax (B) an eye (C) a corpse (D) a gallows
4. The narrator kills his wife when she
(A) is sleeping (B) threatens to leave him (C) stops him from killing the cat (D) catches him drinking in the cellar
5. What does the narrator do with his wife's corpse?
(A) He burns it. (B) He walls it up in the cellar. (C) He throws it in the well. (D) He buries it in the earth.

Drawing Conclusions
6. You can figure that the narrator will most probably
(A) get drunk (B) go insane (C) get married (D) be executed

Using Your Reason

7. The narrator says that the change in the white spot may be happening in his "fancy." By this he means (A) the white spot looks very fancy (B) he may be only imagining the change (C) everyone else notices the change also (D) the cat is probably just shedding some fur

Identifying the Mood

8. After he kills his wife, the narrator feels (A) untroubled (B) very guilty (C) sorrowful (D) frightened

Reading for Deeper Meaning

9. The author would most agree with which of the following? (A) Drunkenness leads to evil deeds. (B) Drunkenness is harmless. (C) Black cats are witches in disguise. (D) All cat owners are alcoholics.

Thinking it Over

1. What is a "conscience"? What does the narrator say that shows his conscience is bothering him about his cruel deeds?
2. The second cat may be seen as a symbol of revenge. In what ways does the cat act as a revenger?
3. Explain how the police are able to find the corpse. Do you think they would have found it had the narrator not started boasting? Why? What do you think caused him to start boasting? Explain.

The Cask of Amontillado

Finding the Main Idea

1. The author is mostly interested in telling how

(A) two men argue about fine wines (B) people celebrate during carnival time (C) the bones of the dead lie peacefully (D) one man gets revenge against another

Remembering Detail
2. What has Fortunato done to the narrator, Montresor?
(A) Insulted him (B) Robbed him (C) Lied to him (D) Tried to kill him
3. Fortunato prides himself on being
(A) an escape artist (B) a master of insults (C) a good judge of wine (D) a person who can see into the future
4. What is Montresor carrying under his cloak?
(A) A gun (B) A knife (C) A trowel (D) The cask of amontillado
5. What does Montresor do to Fortunato deep in the catacombs?
(A) He stabs him. (B) He offers him a bargain. (C) He chains him to a wall. (D) He gives him the amontillado.

Drawing Conclusions
6. You can figure out that after the story, Montresor
(A) feels extremely guilty (B) lives for many years (C) returns and frees Fortunato (D) is arrested and executed

Using Your Reason
7. At one point, the narrator says, "Fortunato was a quack in painting and gems." He would have meant the same thing if he had said that Fortunato
(A) knew nothing about painting and gems (B) was an artist and a jeweler (C) loved to paint pictures of ducks (D) hated paintings and gems
8. Montresor has told Fortunato about the amontillado because Montresor wants to
(A) drink the wine with a friend (B) lure Fortunato into the catacombs (C) get Fortunato's expert opinion

on the wine   (D) find out how much the wine is worth

Identifying the Mood
9. More than anything else, Montresor feels
   (A) sad   (B) determined   (C) forgiving   (D) carefree

Reading for Deeper Meaning
10. Montresor would most agree with which of the following?
    (A) Forgive and forget.   (B) Thou shalt not kill.
    (C) Love your enemy.   (D) Let no one insult you.

Thinking it Over
1. Is there really a cask of amontillado? How do you know?
2. Montresor seems to try to discourage Fortunato from coming along with him to the catacombs. Why does Montresor urge Fortunato to go back?
3. What do you think is the author's purpose in having this story take place during carnival time? How does the fact that it is carnival time aid Montresor in his plan?
4. When the chained Fortunato starts screaming, Montresor is at first afraid. Why? Why does Montresor stop being afraid? How does he show he is no longer afraid?
5. How does the author foreshadow or hint at what Montresor has planned for Fortunato?

A Descent into the Maelstrom

Finding the Main Idea
1. The story is mostly about
   (A) how two brothers die at sea   (B) how to fish off the coast of Norway   (C) how a man survives a terrifying ordeal   (D) how to dive off a cliff overlooking the ocean

Remembering Detail

2. Why did the brothers fish near the Maelstrom?
   (A) They enjoyed dangerous work. (B) The whirlpool could not harm them. (C) There was no place else to fish. (D) There is good fishing in rough water.
3. How long is the period of slack water at the Maelstrom?
   (A)Five minutes (B) Fifteen minutes (C) Two hours (D) Six hours
4. What happened that caused the ship to head into the whirlpool?
   (A) A hurricane came up. (B) A whale charged at the ship. (C) The brothers caught too many fish. (D) The brothers argued among themselves.
5. The fisherman finally saves himself by
   (A) swimming directly into the heart of the whirlpool (B) getting into a lifeboat and rowing away (C) hanging onto a ringbolt near the mast (D) jumping into the water and holding onto a water cask

Drawing Conclusions

6. You can figure that the fisherman is probably about
   (A) 18 years old (B) 25 years old (C) 40 years old (D) 70 years old

Using Your Reason

7. In English, the word *maelstrom* means
   (A) calmness (B) coldness (C) turmoil (D) wisdom
8. The fisherman leaves the ship because
   (A) the whirlpool has stopped (B) a smaller object would go down more slowly than a larger (C) he is afraid of his brother (D) he is a strong swimmer and can escape from the whirlpool

Identifying the Mood

9. As the fisherman and his companion sit at the top of Mount Helseggen, the companion feels

(A) awe-struck and terrified (B) joyous and peaceful
(C) angry and defiant (D) tired and sad

Reading for Deeper Meaning
10. The author would most agree with which of the following?
    (A) Against the forces of nature, humans are very tiny.
    (B) The sea is like a mother, protecting her children.
    (C) A smart sailor never abandons ship. (D) Love for one's brother is stronger than the will to survive.

Thinking it Over
1. What is terror? Do you think it is only fear of death, or is it something else besides? What? How does Poe convey the fisherman's terror to the reader?
2. Have you ever been faced with a terrifying situation? If so, how did you react? If you haven't, how do you think you would react?
3. Why do you suppose the fisherman has taken his companion to the top of Mount Helseggen? Do you think the companion believes the story? Why or why not?

The Fall of the House of Usher

Finding the Main Idea
1. The story is mostly about
   (A) two men's friendship (B) a visitor in an old house
   (C) a man's love for his sister (D) a man's final, fearful days

Remembering Detail
2. On the outside wall of the house, the narrator sees
   (A) bright, silver nails (B) strong, new woodwork
   (C) a long, zigzag crack (D) bricks painted with a strange design

3. Roderick Usher says that he suffers from all of these EXCEPT
   (A) too keen senses (B) fear of danger (C) fear of terror (D) a case of nerves
4. What is wrong with Roderick Usher's sister, Lady Madeline?
   (A) Chills and fever (B) A case of nerves (C) A sickness of the heart (D) An unknown illness
5. Where does Roderick Usher put his sister's body?
   (A) In a vault (B) In his room (C) In the lake (D) In the family burial place
6. At the end of the story, the mansion
   (A) burns to the ground (B) collapses into the lake (C) is bought by the narrator (D) gets a fresh coat of paint

Drawing Conclusions
7. You can figure out that Roderick Usher has never married because he
   (A) has no friends (B) has never met any young women (C) wants the Usher family to die out (D) is afraid to leave his house

Using Your Reason
8. When the narrator says that Roderick Usher's "reason was tottering," he means that Usher
   (A) was very happy (B) was very sad (C) was losing his mind (D) easily lost his balance when walking

Identifying the Mood
9. Which of the following best describes the narrator's mood in the beginning of the story?
   (A) Gloomy (B) Insane (C) Silly (D) Fearful
10. What does Usher feel as the door opens to reveal his sister?
    (A) Terror (B) Joy (C) Love (D) Sadness

11. The author would most agree with which of the following?
    (A) Fear can destroy the ability to reason. (B) There is great happiness in helping a friend. (C) A house dies when its owner dies. (D) Love and fear are the same thing.

Thinking it Over
1. What is the overall mood of this story? How does Poe set up the mood at the very beginning of the story?
2. When the two men are in the vault with the body of Lady Madeline, how does the author foreshadow or hint that she might still be alive?
3. At what point in the story does Roderick Usher realize that his sister is alive? Why doesn't he "dare" say anything about it? What is he afraid of?
4. Explain the double meaning in the title of the story. The third paragraph of the story gives a clue.

The Pit and the Pendulum

Finding the Main Idea
1. The author is mostly interested in telling about
   (A) how a man was tortured and almost killed (B) how prisoners usually escape from jail (C) justice in the Middle Ages (D) a rescue made by rats

Remembering Detail
2. In what city does the story take place?
   (A) Rome (B) Toledo (C) Paris (D) London
3. When the narrator first wakes up in the dungeon, he sees
   (A) a huge pit (B) paintings on the walls (C) total darkness (D) a pendulum

4. At the end of the pendulum is a
   (A) confession for the narrator to sign (B) loaded pistol (C) smooth, wooden ball (D) sharp, steel blade

5. How does the narrator get free from the bands which tie him down?
   (A) General Lasalle cuts him free. (B) The rats chew through them. (C) The pendulum cuts through them. (D) He breaks them with his hands.

6. The walls of the dungeon do all of these EXCEPT
   (A) begin to glow (B) turn red hot (C) close in (D) crumble and fall

Drawing Conclusions

7. After the narrator drops something into the pit, a door opens and shuts above him. You can guess that his torturers are
   (A) giving him a chance to escape (B) leaving more food for him (C) looking to see if he has fallen in (D) putting more rats into the dungeon

Using Your Reason

8. The dungeon is supposed to represent
   (A) the horrors of hell (B) the love of God (C) mercy and forgiveness (D) the narrator's evil mind

9. The reason the food is highly seasoned is to
   (A) attract the rats to it (B) keep the rats away from it (C) increase the thirst of the person eating it (D) cause the person eating it to pass out

Identifying the Mood

10. How does the narrator feel as the rats climb upon him?
    (A) Disgusted but determined not to move (B) Happy that the rats will set him free (C) Sad and ready to accept death (D) Angry that all his food is now gone

Reading for Deeper Meaning

11. The story suggests that human beings
    (A) are just like rats (B) hate to see people suffer
    (C) are always ready to forgive wrongdoers (D) are
    capable of great evil

Thinking it Over

1. What kind of person does the narrator seem to be?
   Why do you suppose he was condemned to die? What
   do you think his crime was?
2. What do you think is in the pit? Does the story give
   you any idea? If so, what?
3. The story is supposed to have taken place during the
   Middle Ages. Do you think people today are capable
   of torturing other people so horribly? Explain your
   answer.

The Angel of the Odd

Finding the Main Idea

1. The story is mostly about a man who
   (A) is careless about fire (B) gets drunk and has some
   very odd dreams (C) has a visitor who teaches him how
   to fly (D) breaks his clock and misses an important
   appointment

Remembering Detail

2. What makes the narrator start thinking about "odd
   accidents"?
   (A) An angel (B) A broken clock (C) A fire in his
   bedroom (D) A newspaper article
3. What or whom does the Angel of the Odd look like?
   (A) The narrator (B) A short man with huge wings
   (C) An ordinary man or woman (D) A collection of
   casks and bottles

4. What happens to the narrator's trousers?
   (A) They fall into the river. (B) A huge hog tears them apart. (C) A drunken crow flies off with them. (D) The Angel of the Odd sets them on fire.
5. Where does the narrator finally awaken?
   (A) On the floor of his bedroom (B) In the office of the insurance company (C) On the dining room hearth (D) In the home of the Angel of the Odd

Drawing Conclusions
6. You can tell from the story that the Angel of the Odd is really
   (A) an insurance man in disguise (B) the narrator's pet dog (C) the narrator's servant (D) a part of the narrator's dream

Using Your Reason
7. When the narrator speaks of his "shining pate," he means his
   (A) bald head (B) clean clothes (C) sparkling silverware (D) empty wine bottle

Identifying the Mood
8. At the very beginning of the story, the narrator is feeling
   (A) sad (B) sober (C) stupid (D) alert
9. Which of the following best describes the character of the Angel of the Odd?
   (A) Argumentative (B) Friendly (C) Boring (D) Even-tempered

Reading for Deeper Meaning
10. The story suggests that
    (A) odd things never happen (B) too much alcohol makes a person foolish (C) dreams usually come true (D) it is wise to believe in angels

215

Thinking it Over

1. Do you believe that the story is a dream? Why or why not?
2. Why do you suppose the Angel of the Odd was made up of wine casks and bottles?
3. What sort of accent is the Angel of the Odd supposed to have? Why does the author give him an accent? What does the accent do to the tone of the story? If the Angel of the Odd did not have an accent, would the story be more serious? sadder? funnier? Why do you say so?

William Wilson

Finding the Main Idea

1. The author is mostly interested in telling how
(A) a boy grows to be a man (B) a man travels around the world (C) a man battles with his conscience
(D) two men with the same name become friends

Remembering Detail

2. The narrator describes himself as being a boy who was
(A) self-willed (B) poor in schoolwork (C) easily controlled by others (D) friendly and loving
3. All of the following are true about the second William Wilson EXCEPT that he
(A) speaks in a whisper (B) looks like the first William Wilson (C) likes to advise the first William Wilson
(D) is a year older than the first William Wilson
4. As a student at Oxford, the narrator
(A) becomes a gambler and a cheat (B) kills a rich young man (C) is a first-rate student (D) decides to become a pastor
5. The second William Wilson appears whenever the narrator

(A) asks him to visit   (B) is down in his luck   (C) is about to cause harm   (D) goes home to see his parents

Drawing Conclusions
6. You can figure out that the two William Wilsons are really
(A) good friends   (B) a man and his son   (C) two parts of the same person   (D) brothers

Using Your Reason
7. When the narrator said "I fled in vain" from the second William Wilson, the narrator would have meant the same thing if he had said that he
(A) was too vain   (B) couldn't get away from the second Wilson   (C) escaped from the second Wilson easily   (D) fled on a train
8. When the second William Wilson says, "You have won and I give up. . . .You are dead to the world," he means that the narrator
(A) had actually killed himself   (B) has destroyed whatever good was left in himself   (C) has finally won the money he always wanted   (D) will be happy for the rest of his life

Identifying the Mood
9. Which of the following best describes the character of the narrator?
(A) Warm and caring   (B) Scornful and unrepentent   (C) Sorrowful and weak   (D) Light-hearted and friendly

Reading for Deeper Meaning
10. The story suggests that if you haven't got a conscience, you
(A) are as good as dead   (B) are very lucky   (C) can do no wrong   (D) have nothing to worry about

Thinking it Over
1. Is there anything in the story which makes you believe that the two William Wilsons are really two different people? Explain your answer.
2. Does the basic idea of the story change if the two William Wilsons are two different people? Why or why not?
3. The narrator says that the second William Wilson "crossed my path only to prevent my carrying out plans that would cause bitter harm. But this was a poor excuse for taking away my natural rights to lead my own life in my own way." Do you agree with the narrator on what he says about his "natural rights"? Why or why not? What are "natural rights"?

Never Bet the Devil Your Head

Finding the Main Idea
1. Which title tells most about the story?
(A) "Toby's Terrible Mother" (B) "The Day I Met the Devil" (C) "The Sad Life and Death of Toby" (D) "The Reform of a Betting Man"

Remembering Detail
2. When Toby was small, his mother
(A) beat him (B) gave him too much candy (C) sent him away (D) made him do the cooking
3. The narrator tries to
(A) jump over a turnstile (B) stop Toby from betting (C) keep Toby's mother away from him (D) bet the devil Toby's head
4. The little old gentleman is wearing
(A) Toby's hat (B) a yellow suit (C) a black silk apron (D) a black silk tie
5. Toby hits his head against

(A) a window (B) the turnstile (C) the wall of the bridge (D) an iron brace

Drawing Conclusions
6. You can guess that the little old gentleman is really
   (A) the devil (B) Toby's father (C) the narrator
   (D) Toby's conscience

Using Your Reason
7. When the narrator said "Toby was in high spirits," he would have meant the same thing if he had said that Toby was
   (A) feeling bad (B) seeing ghosts (C) drinking a lot
   (D) enjoying himself

Identifying the Mood
8. How does Toby feel after he hears the word "ahem"?
   (A) Sad (B) Happy (C) Angry (D) Mean
9. When the author wrote this story he was probably feeling
   (A) sincere (B) scornful (C) down-hearted (D) humorous

Reading for Deeper Meaning
10. The author would most agree with which of the following?
    (A) Only bet on a sure thing. (B) Don't jump in a dark place. (C) Don't trust anyone who says "ahem."
    (D) You're crazy if you believe this story.

Thinking it Over
1. While the old gentleman waited for Toby to jump, he "looked up" and "tightened the strings of his apron." What do you think was his reason for doing this?
2. Do you consider this a humorous story? Why or why not?

3. What are some of the ridiculous things that happen in this story? Why are they ridiculous?

Three Sundays in a Week

Finding the Main Idea
1. The author is mostly interested in telling how Bobby and Kate
   (A) find a way to get married (B) first decide to get married (C) act when they are married (D) decide not to get married

Remembering Detail
2. In what city does this story take place?
   (A) Rome (B) Cairo (C) Havana (D) London
3. Kate will marry Bobby whenever
   (A) he can get enough money (B) his great-uncle says "yes" (C) he returns from a trip around the world (D) a Sunday falls on a Wednesday
4. Captain Smitherton and Captain Pratt traveled
   (A) in opposite directions (B) on the same ship (C) on different ships in the same direction (D) first north, then south
5. The earth spins from
   (A) south to north (B) north to south (C) west to east (D) east to west

Drawing Conclusions
6. You can tell from the story that the great-uncle
   (A) dislikes Bobby greatly (B) never drinks any alcohol (C) enjoys word games (D) wishes he had been in the navy

Using Your Reason
7. By saying his great-uncle has "a long purse," Bobby means his great-uncle is
   (A) angry (B) poor (C) rude (D) wealthy

8. By saying that his great-uncle acted "like an old mouser
. . . toward us two poor mice," Bobby means that his
great-uncle
(A) looks like a fat cat (B) liked to tease Bobby and
Kate (C) was really very patient (D) didn't want
Bobby and Kate to marry

Identifying the Mood

9. At the beginning of the story, how does Bobby feel
toward his great-uncle?
(A) Happy (B) Angry (C) Loving (D) Grateful
10. The great-uncle is both stubborn and
(A) mean (B) generous (C) unhappy (D) foolish

Reading for Deeper Meaning

11. Which of the following does the great-uncle value most?
(A) Keeping one's word to the letter (B) Allowing
people to do as they wish (C) Being serious at all times
(D) Living quietly and soberly

Thinking it Over

1. Has Captain Smitherton aged two more days than
Captain Pratt during the past year? Why or why not?
2. Describe the character of the old man, Bobby's great-
uncle. Why do you think he acts the way he does?
3. Sometimes people faced with many restrictions find a
loophole so they can do what they want. Have you ever
used a loophole to be able to do what you wanted? Explain your answer.

The System of Dr. Tarr and
Prof. Fether

Finding the Main Idea

1. The author is mostly interested in telling about
(A) a new system for treating mental patients (B) a

young man who attends an interesting dinner party
(C) mental patients who take over a mental hospital
(D) some violent men who escape from a mental hospital

Remembering Detail

2. The narrator describes himself as being a
   (A) lawyer (B) medical student (C) "human top"
   (D) madman
3. Under the "soothing system," patients were treated as if they
   (A) were wealthy ladies and gentlemen (B) were violent criminals (C) were in their right minds
   (D) knew they were mad
4. It turns out that Superintendent Maillard
   (A) has himself gone crazy (B) had left the madhouse weeks ago (C) is disguised as one of the patients (D) is locked up in a cell
5. The men who break into the dining room are really
   (A) the keepers (B) big baboons (C) the musicians
   (D) madmen

Drawing Conclusions

6. You can figure out that Superintendent Maillard believes that the narrator is
   (A) mad (B) clever (C) stupid (D) brilliant

Using Your Reason

7. The young woman who is dressed "in deep mourning" is probably wearing
   (A) blue (B) yellow (C) white (D) black
8. The narrator's main reason for visiting the madhouse is to
   (A) rescue the keepers (B) warn Superintendent Maillard that the police are coming (C) have dinner with Superintendent Maillard (D) learn about the "soothing system"

Identifying the Mood

9. When the keepers break into the dinner party, the diners become
   (A) very calm   (B) obviously "crazy"   (C) furious
   (D) sad

Reading for Deeper Meaning

10. The character of Superintendent Maillard shows that a crazy person may also be
    (A) sane   (B) clever   (C) evil   (D) lucky

Thinking it Over

1. Why do the keepers look like baboons? What is tarring and feathering? What is the "system" of Dr. Tarr and Prof. Fether?
2. When did you realize that the diners were really the patients? What clues did you have? When did you first suspect that Superintendent Maillard was mad? What clues did you have?
3. Why does the narrator believe Superintendent Maillard? What is there about Maillard's actions and conversation that makes him so believable?
4. What is your opinion of the narrator? When do you think he realizes the truth? Should he have realized it sooner? Why or why not?

The Spectacles

Finding the Main Idea

1. The author is mostly interested in telling how a young man
   (A) decides to buy himself a pair of glasses   (B) meets and marries a woman older than himself   (C) gets a new last name   (D) spends an evening at the opera

Remembering Detail

2. At the opera, Simpson falls in love with
   (A) the sister of his friend Talbot (B) the young Stéphanie Lalande (C) a woman twice his age (D) a woman he can hardly see

3. The day after the opera, Simpson's friend Talbot
   (A) leaves town (B) introduces him to Madame Lalande (C) gives him a pair of glasses (D) offers to lend him a thousand dollars

4. Simpson believes that Madame Lalande is
   (A) 27 years old (B) 45 years old (C) 63 years old (D) 82 years old

5. Madame Lalande turns out to be
   (A) 90 years old (B) a friend of the family (C) Simpson's great-great-grandmother (D) Simpson's mother's cousin

Drawing Conclusions

6. You can tell that Madame Eugénie Lalande marries Simpson in order to
   (A) get his money (B) take him back to Paris (C) teach him a lesson (D) prove that she is still attractive

Using Your Reason

7. When the author says that Madame Lalande is "a great catch," he would have meant the same thing if he had said that she
   (A) has just come from Paris (B) would be a good person to marry (C) is a lively talker (D) is a fine athlete

8. When Madame Lalande says, "Don't buy a pig in a poke," she means
   (A) a pig is a poor bargain (B) don't buy a farm if you're not a farmer (C) never fall in love at first sight (D) don't buy something you can't see

Identifying the Mood

9. After Simpson finds out how old Madame Lalande is, how does she speak to him?
   (A) Hatefully (B) Joyfully (C) Sweetly (D) Mockingly

Reading for Deeper Meaning

10. The story suggests that people can act foolishly because of
    (A) vanity (B) shyness (C) greed (D) fear

Thinking it Over

1. Explain the misunderstanding at the opera house. Why is Simpson staring at Madame Lalande? Why does she stare back at him? How does each misinterpret the other's actions? Whom does Talbot think Simpson is staring at?

2. How does Poe explain the circumstance of a man having a great-great-grandmother who is "only" 60 years older than himself?

3. What lesson does Napoleon Bonaparte Froissart Simpson learn? Do you think it is a good lesson? Why or why not?

The Raven

Thinking it Over

1. In one of his essays, Poe told how he wrote "The Raven." He wanted to write a poem with a tone of sadness. What things about the poem do you think were intended to give it a tone of sadness?

2. Poe's poems are famous mainly because of the *sound* of the words he used. After you have read "The Raven" silently a few times, try reading it out loud. Do you like

it better when you actually hear it, or when you just read it?

3. Several kinds of birds can be trained to mimic human speech. Why do you think Poe chose to use a raven instead of a parrot, for example? Would the tone of sadness remain if you used *parrot* instead of *raven* in the poem?

The Bells

Thinking it Over

1. The first stanza of "The Bells" describes the jingling sound of silver sleigh bells. What words does the author use to imitate the light, rapid, merry sound of sleigh bells?

2. The second stanza of this poem describes the sound of wedding bells. What words in this stanza express the happiness of a wedding? Can you think of any other words Poe could have used?

3. The third stanza of "The Bells" describes the sound of alarm bells. What words does the author use to make you think of harsh, loud sounds?

4. The last stanza describes funeral bells. What words does the poet use to express grief or sadness? What other words could he have used?

Annabel Lee

Thinking it Over

1. In "Annabel Lee" Poe does not tell us very much about his love. What or where is "this kingdom by the sea"? Who are the "highborn kinsmen"? What did Annabel Lee really die of?

El Dorado

Thinking it Over
1. What do you think a "gallant knight gayly bedight" would look like? What kind of costume would he wear?
2. What two conditions cause the knight to become discouraged?
3. What do you think the "shadow" means when it tells the knight to go "Over the Mountains Of the Moon, Down the Valley of the Shadow" to find El Dorado? Where is El Dorado?

Sonnet to Science

Thinking it Over
1. In "Sonnet to Science" the poet seems to be complaining that science has caused people to be concerned only with facts. He seems to think that science has made people lose their imaginations and feelings. This poem was first published in 1849. How do you think Poe would feel about science today? Would you agree or disagree with him? Why?
2. A sonnet is a poem of 14 lines that deals with only one subject. The measure (number of syllables in each line) and the rhyme pattern can vary from poem to poem. Read "Sonnet to Science" silently a few times. Find the rhyme pattern and the measure. Then see if you can write your own sonnet.

To Helen

Thinking it Over
1. "To Helen" is a strangely mixed expression of love

for a person and love for all that is classic. Many songs and poems have been written comparing a person to something in nature. Think of someone you would like to write a song or poem to. What would you compare that person to? Why?